WELL-BEING
AT
WORK

WELL-BEING
AT
WORK

*How to Experience
Rewarding Employment by
Maximizing Your Value*

GARRETT G. TERHUNE

Published by Maximum Positive Impact, Inc.
104 Locust Ave.
Red Bank, NJ 07701
www.MPimpact.com

ISBN Paperback: 978-0-9973025-0-9
ISBN eBook: 978-0-9973025-2-3

Library of Congress Control Number: 2016906222
LCCN Imprint Name: Red Bank, NJ

*To people around the world who desire
the well-being that good, satisfying work enables.*

Contents

Preface

Memories of our lives, of our works and
our deeds will continue in others.
—Rosa Parks

T his book is about increasing your likelihood of staying gainfully employed.

This book provides core, specific actions you need to take to maximize and maintain your value in the global workforce. Sometimes it's the smallest advantage that can make a major difference. You should carefully consider any honorable advantage you can gain to better position yourself in the global marketplace.

Four stirring realities inspired me to write this book.

1. Being gainfully employed is paramount to experiencing an overall sense of well-being in one's life. In addition, when human beings

are applying their efforts toward a positive, worthy ideal, *every stage of life is positively affected.* Accomplishments abound!

2. All learning opportunities are *not* equal in their effectiveness. All coaching opportunities are *not* equal in their effectiveness. Therefore, everyone is not getting an equal opportunity to perform. Training and coaching *inconsistency* and *ineffectiveness* abound.

   This is unacceptable. Livelihoods are at stake. Well-being is at stake.

3. In his eye-opening book *The Coming Jobs War,* Jim Clifton, chairman of Gallup Corporation, makes the following statement:

   "What the whole world wants is a good job. This is one of the most important discoveries Gallup has ever made. A *good* job is a job with a paycheck from an employer and steady work that averages 30 + hours per week."

   He goes on to state that at the time his book was written,
   - the global population was 7 billion;
   - of these, 5 billion were adults aged fifteen or older;
   - of those, 3 billion told Gallup they work or want to work; and
   - there were 1.2 billion full-time, formal jobs in the world.

   Clifton said that "this leaves a global shortfall of *1.8 billion* good jobs. At the same time, global unemployment was approaching 50 percent."

   I find it tragic and disturbing that there are so few jobs for so many people who want to work.

4. There is so much unrest in our world when it comes to lack of work, and I believe this is the root of many of society's problems. I also think that much of the violence in our world today stems from people's feelings of not belonging. People need to belong to *something*. They join groups to belong. If they can't find gainful employment, they seek out other "solutions" for their need. I believe this is a major reason that people turn to terrorism. They are angry. They are frustrated. They are financially deprived. They need to take out their frustrations. So they join others with these same frustrations, which are released in very destructive, harmful ways.

And we wonder why there is so much unrest and gnashing of teeth on our planet.

This book is my attempt to help relieve some of the unrest.

People who have something better to do with their time, such as actively participating in the global supply chain (in other words, having good, satisfying work), are less likely to get involved in negative or destructive activities. All countries need to be active contributors to the global supply chain of goods and services. Once they are involved as an important link in the chain, people, businesses, and countries won't want to ruin a good thing. When life is good, people are more likely to calm down and settle into a peaceful lifestyle.

If more people could become employed as part of the global supply chain, I believe it would be a major positive movement toward a more peaceful, happier, healthier, and safer world.

If you've ever wondered, "What can *I* do to make a difference in contributing to a better world," I've got something for you to do.

As you'll read in chapter 8, "A Strategy for Creating Jobs," *each and every one of us* can contribute to getting people employed. Each and every one of us can contribute to making this a more peaceful, happier, healthier, and safer world.

Maximum Positive Impact— More Than Just a Company Name

Maximum Positive Impact, Inc. is our company name. But maximum positive impact is more than just a company name. It is our aspiration for you. And what a noble aspiration it is—to have a maximum positive impact on everyone you meet—to have maximum positive impact on the world around you. Having maximum positive impact on your employer, your family, your community, and our planet is a wonderful contribution. Think of each word and the significance each word carries. You will see the words maximum positive impact throughout this book.

Why We at Maximum Positive Impact, Inc. Do What We Do

We exist to help relieve the worldwide epidemic of joblessness and the despair it causes.

Gainfully employed individuals are happier, healthier individuals. Happier, healthier individuals lead to
- happier, healthier families;
- happier, healthier communities;

- happier, healthier countries; and ultimately
- a happier, healthier, safer planet.

We care deeply about the overall well-being of our planet and the people and creatures that inhabit it.

When I say "we," I don't just mean those of us at Maximum Positive Impact, Inc. I mean *you, me,* and *all* who buy into our mission of *helping to relieve the worldwide epidemic of joblessness and the despair it causes* and of working together toward a worthy ideal.

You at work. *A world* at work. A truly worthy ideal.

Let's start with *you* being gainfully employed. Then, let's all contribute to getting others gainfully employed as well. In chapter 8, you'll learn how you can contribute to this noble cause by simply being at your best every day.

What We Do

We help *individuals* increase the likelihood of
- finding good, satisfying work;
- keeping good, satisfying work;
- finding better, satisfying work; and
- participating in a noble cause by helping others find and keep good or better satisfying work.

As a residual effect, we help *organizations* increase the likelihood of
- employing engaged, productive, valuable employees;
- creating more jobs by retaining and attaining more customers; and

- maximizing the return on all of their learning initiatives by making all their training and coaching efforts more effective.

How We Do It

We empower people in the area of well-being at work by teaching and coaching people on *how to experience rewarding employment by maximizing their value.*

This book is about helping you achieve well-being at work. *Well-Being at Work*, along with being the title of this book, is a proprietary product delivered by Maximum Positive Impact, Inc. It is a concept that encompasses the actions of learning, following through, and performing. These three actions, along with the right mind-set, performed with maximum positive impact increase the likelihood of you finding and keeping good, satisfying work and its accompanying compensation. One of the wonderful residual effects of such work is the major contribution it makes to your overall well-being.

The core competencies in this book increase the likelihood that you will

- *truly acquire* essential knowledge and skills throughout your career;
- convert knowledge and skills into high-quality, on-the-job performance; and
- sustain performance excellence over time.

For Whom This Book Is Intended

This book is written for you, the individual.

For you the worker or you the aspiring worker.

For you, the contributor to the global supply chain.

Maybe you have a title, maybe not. Maybe you work in an office or on a factory floor or in a retail store. Perhaps you work outside. Maybe you wear a white collar; maybe you wear a blue collar. Perhaps you are a contractor, a freelancer, or an independent consultant. You might own or aspire to own your own business. You might be currently working. You might be currently looking for work.

This book is for anyone who is of working age or approaching working age and wants to work and wants to continue working.*

You, the Performer

Throughout this book, I refer to you as a *performer*. You are all performers, even though you are variously called employees, talent, human capital, and so on. I call you performers because the bottom line is that you must *perform* to sustain your livelihood.

Your Roles as a Performer

As a performer, you have several roles. First and foremost, you are an *on-the-job performer* who must perform the responsibilities and tasks of your work with sustained excellence. You as a performer will also continuously play the role of *learner*. As a learner, you must perform during learning engagements as a responsible, active learner. Also, as a performer, you will always play the role of *coachee*. You will be one who follows through to stay progressive and who pursues mastery of key skills and responsibilities. During follow-through activities, you must actively perform to make the very most of those opportunities.

Global Competition

I call you a *performer* in your various roles because that is exactly who you must be to survive in today's global workforce. And yes, I do mean global. People around the world are craving your job. They are working to win your customers away from you. With today's robust, immediate communications capabilities, your competitors can be anywhere in the world. So, yes, when you are sleeping, there are those on the other side of the world who are awake and desiring your job and your customers. They are actively doing everything they can to take it all away from you.

You must not sit idly by and allow this to happen. You can't just leave it to chance and see what transpires. You must be proactive in maximizing and maintaining your value in the global workforce. Be *highly* proactive. Convert the knowledge and skills you've learned and maintained through training and coaching into stellar on-the-job performance. You must consistently *perform with excellence* to remain an active participant in the global workforce.

I have aspirations for you well beyond *just* performing, though. I see you *excelling*. I see you being an invaluable contributor to your employer and to the world of commerce at large. I see you setting a new standard of excellence for your profession. I see you being *the* go-to person in your area of expertise. I see you reveling in the well-being that gainful employment brings.

*Note: If you are not yet old enough to work (or you know someone who is not yet of working age) but want to become a voracious, first-class learner, read the chapters on "How to *Learn* with Maximum Positive Impact" and "How to *Follow Through* with Maximum Positive Impact."

A Few Notes About This Book

Nowadays only brutally simple ideas get through.

—Daniel H. Pink

I've attempted to say what needs to be said in as few words as possible. This is not meant to be an endless tome. Where focus points (•) sufficed, they (as opposed to sentences or paragraphs) were used. This book is also *not* meant to be a breakthrough in the science of adult learning. Rather, it is a series of lessons, observations, personal experiences, and personal learning and study that I have accrued over more than forty years in business. The writing is based on firsthand experience, not merely theory. I have written this book to help you reach the peak of your capabilities. Use it as a reference guide.

- When you have a pending learning opportunity, review chapter 5, "How to *Learn* with Maximum Positive Impact."

- Immediately prior to a coaching session, revisit "How to *Follow Through* with Maximum Positive Impact" in chapter 6.

- Continuously review "How to *Perform* with Maximum Positive Impact" in chapter 7 until it becomes part of your personal brand.

- Refer often to the Maximum Positive Impact *Pillars of Well-Being at Work* in chapter 4 for guidance and inspiration.

- Frequently revisit "A Strategy for Creating Jobs" in chapter 8 to strengthen your resolve and to remind yourself you are contributing to a greater purpose.

Pssst…I've got a secret…

The Secret Ingredient

There is a secret ingredient that must be in the mix, or this cake won't rise. The secret ingredient? *Caring.* You must *care deeply* about achieving well-being at work. You must care deeply about providing for your family. You must care deeply about your and your family's overall well-being.

If you are more interested in just getting by, if you are only interested in doing just enough so that you don't get fired, this book is not for you. This book is for people who have a burning desire for well-being.

If someone were to ask me, "What is the *one thing* that sets you apart from others in your industry?" I wouldn't hesitate to answer. It's *caring.* I've always cared deeply about my performance. I won't allow myself to fail. I've always had a deep fear of failure, so I wasn't going to allow it to happen. I've always cared deeply about my customers. Caring has served me well, and it can be a *huge* differentiator for you, too. Care deeply, and you won't go wrong. Plus, it's good for the soul!

Join me in caring deeply.

The quality of a person's life is in direct proportion to their commitment to excellence, regardless of their chosen field of endeavor.
—Vince Lombardi

Happy learning!

Introduction

Between stimulus and response, there is a space.
In that space is our power to choose our response. In our response
lies our growth and our freedom.
—Victor Frankl

Well-being. Being well. Happiness. We all pursue it. When you think of the word *well-being*, what does it mean to you? What does it *look* like for you? What does it *feel* like? Perhaps it includes

- provision for your family,
- easily met financial obligations,
- financial security,
- health,
- love,
- recreation,

1

- spiritual beliefs,
- ownership and maintenance of a home, and
- _____ (you fill in the blank).

These are just a few of the manifestations of well-being. More than likely though, it's a combination of the above…and more. Perhaps you are experiencing well-being right now. Or perhaps well-being is currently just a dream of how your future can be. Everyone craves it. We all pursue it in one way or another. It can be and often is *elusive*.

When you do secure it, it *feels* wonderful. It means you are living a balanced, happy, rewarding life. It means you've got your priorities straight. Well-being is truly a worthy aspiration.

One key area of your overall well-being is your ability to maintain a steady income while enjoying good, satisfying work. Good, satisfying work is about offering a valuable service to others and feeling great about doing so. It's about the satisfaction and peace of mind that accompany earning a solid week's pay.

If good, satisfying work and that weekly pay are missing, your overall well-being is severely affected, unless you happen to be independently wealthy. I would go so far as to say that without such work and pay, overall well-being is virtually impossible.

When you are gainfully employed, approximately 25 percent of your time is spent at work. But so many people are unhappy in their work. Too many are working just in anticipation of the weekend. Suffering through 25 percent of your life is too dear a price to pay. It affects all other aspects of your life.

Time Keeps on Ticking, Ticking, Ticking

The lessons this book offers will help you *fill your days* with meaningful, satisfying activities and experiences, because

- minutes turn into hours;
- hours turn into days;
- days turn into weeks;
- weeks turn into months; and
- months turn into years.

Before you know it, you have...a *lifetime*. When you look back, you'll realize the hours that comprised those days, the minutes that made up those hours, and the seconds that ticked away in those minutes were (and continue to be) life itself. Well-being is about filling your day, *today*, with worthwhile activities and experiences.

Now is life. The past is a memory. The future is a dream.

Enjoy *now*. Enjoy the journey. Enjoy the successes. Experience, endure, and learn from the challenges and obstacles. Experience *you* having maximum positive impact on the world around you.

What Is Well-Being at Work?

Well-being at work starts with *being gainfully employed*—having good, satisfying work and being paid fairly for the value you bring to your employer. Complementary attributes include the following:

- the *satisfaction* of being gainfully employed
- the *relief* of being able to afford the necessities of life
- the *assurance* in knowing you can always provide for your family

- the *pride* associated with always meeting your financial responsibilities
- the *joy* of being able to afford some of the pleasures of life
- the *gratification* associated with making the most of your capabilities and talents
- the *fulfillment* of making a solid contribution to the world's marketplace
- the *pleasure* you feel when you are involved in satisfying and meaningful work
- the *pride* you feel when performing with excellence
- the *peace of mind* that accompanies putting forth your best effort
- the *peace of mind* and the *satisfaction* that accompany consistently getting paid
- the *harmony* you experience when blending with your employer's culture
- the *inner contentment* associated with being a pleasure to work with
- the *security* of knowing you are highly marketable and readily able to adapt to change
- the *satisfaction* of contributing to a purpose bigger than yourself (*knowing* that you are contributing to the overall well-being of our planet)
- the *reassurance* of being valuable (when you are productive, you are valuable, and when you are valuable, you have a tendency to stay gainfully employed)
- the *sanctuary* experienced when all of the above are *your reality*

Well-being is also about *staying* highly employable.

Staying Highly Employable

A huge part of well-being at work is to always *stay highly employable*, knowing that when things change, you will be in a situation that will allow you to get hired quickly into a position commensurate with your talent.

Employable =
Possessing highly marketable and currently valuable skills

Stay employable if you already are. Perhaps you already possess marketable expertise and experience. You are already in an advantageous position. Fantastic! Now, expand your knowledge and skills. Increase your value. Prepare for the change you know is coming, and don't let it blindside you. Read everything you can get your hands on to enhance your knowledge and skills. Take classes. Seek out different opinions and ideas. Measure others' ideas against your own. Do they work for you? Whenever you come across new information, you have a decision to make. Should you use this new information or should you discard it?

Become employable if you're not already. Perhaps you don't yet have a profession, or perhaps you are involved in one that isn't making you happy. You may be looking for something new and perhaps different.

Where are the *needs* out there? What area of need resonates with you? For what profession might you have the necessary aptitude? What profession will you pursue? In what area will you choose to acquire specialized knowledge and skills? Make the decision and then stick with it. Focus. Once you decide on a promising profession, go full speed ahead! Learn, follow through, and then perform. First become employable, and then become employed! This book will help you do just that.

So What Is *Your* Occupational Goal?

What does well-being at work mean to *you* right now? Perhaps it means

- getting good, satisfying work ➲ and basking in the *relief* that accompanies it;
- keeping good, satisfying work ➲ and enjoying the *security* that accompanies it;
- getting better, satisfying work ➲ and reveling in the *triumph* that accompanies it; and
- helping others accomplish the above ➲ and feeling the *satisfaction* that accompanies it.

It's time to take control of your well-being.

There are many different paths to success. As you'll read a little later on, I didn't choose the easiest or the most prestigious path, for sure.

Don't feel you have to change the world in order to succeed. Try to master *your* positive contribution to it, and the world as you experience it will change…for the better.

How To

I probably don't have to sell you on the value of well-being. But sometimes we get so lost, we forget what it feels like. We forget what feeling good feels like.

Often we get advice (from just about everyone) on *what* to do. *How* to do it is left to our own discretion. This book covers three concrete *hows*—three actions you can take to increase the likelihood of getting and keeping good, satisfying work.

These three core actions are

1. learning;
2. following through; and
3. performing.

These three core competencies are the primary focus of this book. You will gain the step-by-step procedures, strategies, and tools to make these core competencies work for you. While there are very few *definites* when it comes to being employed, staying employed, and being employable, these are three concrete actions you can take to *increase the likelihood of experiencing well-being at work*. Combining these three competencies successfully in your life will put you in a powerful position.

OK. So you think all this sounds good. But you may be wondering, who is this Garrett Terhune, and why should I listen to him?

From There to Here

Employ your time in improving yourself by other's writings,
so that you shall gain easily what others have labored hard for.
—Socrates

June 19, 1973

As I opened my eyes and looked straight up into the sky, I saw the last remnants of stars giving way to the morning sunrise.

It was in the early morning hours of June 19, 1973. About a dozen of us had camped out on the front lawn of a classmate's house. The evening before, we had graduated high school. After spending the night celebrating, we'd decided to sleep under the stars rather than make our way home.

As I lay there that morning, I took a deep breath and said, loudly enough so that only I could hear, "What now?" I had *no idea* what to do from that point forward. The only direction I had received up to then had been, "Get a job!" I'd had no other direction or guidance.

So I borrowed a car and drove from factory to factory, from business to business. I'd walk in and announce that I was looking for a job. They'd ask, "What kind of job?"

And I'd answer, "I dunno…any job."

One company offered me a job dipping pieces of metal into acid, all the while covered head to toe in a heavy, sweltering rubber suit. I said yes. Anguishing as I lay on the beach at Seaside Heights, New Jersey, the weekend before I was due to start my new job, I decided that I couldn't bear it. I called on Monday morning and quit my first job before I ever started.

Then, I decided on a new approach—I'd start saying that I was looking for a job in shipping and receiving. One company met with me on the front steps of their offices. "I'm here looking for a job," I proclaimed. Nothing was available. I went back to this company several times, until finally they asked, "Why do you want to work here so much?" I replied, "It's close to home."

This company must have felt sorry for me. They ended up giving me a job in shipping and receiving for $2.75 per hour ($22.00 per day,

$110.00 per week). Many of the products I shipped (hydraulic and pneumatic valves) weighed hundreds of pounds each. Interestingly, they did not have a truck-level shipping dock. These products had to be lifted up to the truck bed with a *hand-cranked* forklift device. It was backbreaking, dangerous work, and it needed to be done in all kinds of weather—heat, cold, snow, sleet, or rain. I had this job for more than three years. One time, they asked me to count pieces of spare parts for an inventory process. I replied, "I don't think I can do that." My confidence in my ability to do almost anything that required any kind of thinking was nonexistent.

Contributing to this lack of confidence was a humiliating experience I once had trying to speak in front of a group of people at school. When I moved my mouth...nothing. No words came out. I was petrified and humiliated. The teacher said, "You can sit down, Garrett." All of my classmates stared at me in wide-eyed silence.

Fast Forward to 2016

For the past thirteen years, I've trained and coached high-level executives for some of the world's most prestigious corporations. I prepare CEOs, CFOs, CIOs, presidents, vice presidents, and other company officials to have greater impact and presence, and to be more effective communicators during major presentations, speeches, and public appearances.

Prior to this, I trained hundreds of people on how to use comprehensive accounting software (remember, I once couldn't even handle counting inventory). I've trained thousands of salespeople on how to increase their productivity through the use of sales techniques, presentation skills, enhanced relationship building, and customer-relationship management software.

I've led thousands of people through various programs throughout the United States and Europe for some of the world's largest enterprises.

I've had colleagues literally waiting in line outside my office door seeking my assistance and advice.

I have worked alongside college professors, people with advanced degrees (most of the positions I've held required advanced degrees), people with years more experience than I had, and people with more intelligence than I had.

And I have more than held my own. As a matter of fact, I was once paired up with a college professor to teach a two-day class, and afterward he said to me, "I was scared to death prior to working with you." I asked, why? He said, "I didn't know if I could keep up."

I tell you all this not to boast or brag but to paint an unlikely picture of how in the world I ended up *here*, where I am now, from *there*, where I started from. It has become a cliché, but, truly, if *I* can do it, *you* can do it.

So what happened in between? There were grueling decades of blood, sweat, and tears. There was a lot of the following:
- educating myself
- studying
- reading
- attending workshops
- desiring

- feeling discomfort
- making mistakes (that cost me thousands of dollars and little chunks of my soul)
- selling myself over and over and over again
- repeatedly performing under intense pressure
- succeeding
- failing
- feeling enthusiasm
- experiencing despondency
- failing in several of my own initiatives
- showing determination
- having discipline
- caring deeply about my performance
- caring deeply about my customers
- finding myself in sink-or-swim situations
- feeling depression
- experiencing hopelessness
- taking chances
- auditioning (for training positions)
- engaging in change—much change

I also had to deal with the following circumstances and life events:

- I have not earned a college degree.
- I endured a difficult marriage that ended in divorce.
- I got caught up in the financial crisis of 2008 and experienced a humiliating personal bankruptcy.
- My wife and I sold a house at a significant financial loss.
- I lived for years without health insurance.

- I've had to rely on unemployment insurance several times in my life.
- I've suffered a broken spirit.
- I've experienced what it's like not being able to eat. In other words, I was penniless. On two occasions in my life, I could not scrape together enough coins to buy a candy bar. I went to bed without having had a bite to eat. Let me tell you, if you've never been there, you never want to go there.
- And, sadly, at times I was so despondent that I couldn't imagine how I could possibly wake up the next morning.

Not exactly a glowing résumé for a writer of a book on well-being, is it?

So, Really, Why in the World *Would* I Listen to Garrett Terhune?

How *am* I qualified to lead you into well-being at work? I'm qualified because I've experienced and learned. Through determination, discipline, focus, and effort I've experienced and learned *what to do* and *how to do it*. I've also learned what *not* to do. I've learned the hard way but the most effective way—through firsthand experience. I've lived it, and I've consistently picked myself up when I didn't think I could.

There are about a million things I am not very good at. But what I *am* good at is delivering when it is time to perform. Prior to "performing" (that is, doing the work), I am always comprehensively prepared. Along with being well prepared I always care deeply about my performance and my customer. I believe my caring, my preparation,

12

and my consistent delivery with *everything that I've got* have been the biggest contributors to the success I've enjoyed.

For the majority of my career, I have for the most part stayed employed, initially with very few credentials. It somehow happened. Well, it didn't really just *somehow* happen—I know how it happened. That's what I'll be sharing with you in this book.

So what got me from *there* to *here*?

Trial and Error = Learning

I have spent decades inching forward one exhausting step at a time. If I didn't like my current position in life, I changed it. When I changed something, however, I always looked to move *upward*. My path to success has looked something like this:

Trial and error = Learning ➲ Adjustment

Trial and error = Learning ➲ Adjustment

Trial and error = Learning ➲ Adjustment

Trial and error = Learning ➲ Adjustment

Trial and error = Learning ➲ Adjustment

Trial and error = Learning ➲ Adjustment

Trial and error = Learning ➲ Adjustment

And, finally, **triumph!**

Notice the word *learning* throughout my journey. Interestingly enough, even though I have never earned a degree from a university, I have been a voracious reader and learner throughout my adolescent and adult life. My learning just hasn't taken the form of attending an accredited learning institution.

A Shorter Journey

My goal is to shorten your journey and speed up your realization of well-being at work, so that your experience looks more like this:

Trial and error = Learning ➲ Adjustment

Trial and error = Learning ➲ Adjustment

Triumph!

This is how to get it right. This is how to succeed. The purpose of this book is to save *you* a lot of time and effort.

During my journey, I learned five essential lessons. This book addresses all of them:

1. Good, satisfying work is essential to one's well-being.
2. All learning opportunities are not equal in their effectiveness.
3. We all need help and support (from a coach or mentor).
4. You must perform or be gone.
5. The *customer* is the key.

Update Upon Completion of the Writing of this Book

Well, I survived. More than that, I am experiencing blissful well-being at work and have done so for many years. I am empowered like never before. So...let's do this. Let's do this together.

PART 1

Chapter 1

A Problem

*There's nothing worse than getting up in the morning
and going to a job you don't like.*
—Gladys Terhune

To paraphrase this nugget of wisdom from my dear grandmother, I believe "there's nothing worse than getting up in the morning and having no job to go to."

A Problem Facing Us in Today's World

For many of us, a key concern is the absence of well-being at work due a lack of good, satisfying work, which can stem from joblessness or job insecurity, among other things.

It is my problem. It is your problem. It is the world's problem.

17

Some of the causes of this lack of good, satisfying work are
- not enough employers and jobs;
- too many people looking for good, satisfying work and not enough jobs to accommodate them;
- people not having a skill set that is in sync with current job requirements;
- automation—machines doing what people used to do; and
- change.

Change

Change comes quickly and often in today's global workplace. Things may be going along smoothly, and then, *boom*, your boss leaves. Everything is clicking along on all cylinders, and then, *boom*, your organization is purchased by another entity. Your organization is thriving, and then, *boom*, a change in technology leaves your organization's products obsolete.

Boom often equals layoffs.

Implications

If one is not gainfully employed, overall well-being is virtually impossible. It affects whether or not you have a roof over your head. It affects your self-esteem. It affects your ability to provide for your family. It affects your relationships. It affects your health. Your occupation affects everything.

I won't apologize for painting a bleak picture here. It is reality. Work deprivation can lead to the following:
- lack of money
- debt

- inability to pay off debt
- insecurity
- hopelessness
- stress
- anxiety
- tension
- pressure
- health issues
- family issues
- despair
- cynicism
- jadedness
- fatigue

In extreme cases, it can result in these circumstances:
- bankruptcy
- homelessness
- violence

And to me, this is the saddest implication:
- a broken spirit

Lost Hope

Most of the important things in the world have been accomplished by people who have kept on trying when there seemed to be no hope at all.
—Dale Carnegie

Global unemployment numbers are approaching 50 percent (as found by the study mentioned earlier in this book). Jim Clifton, chairman of Gallup said that "in America alone, there are 30 million Americans who *don't* have a good job, and 18 million report to Gallup as having no hope of finding a job."

That's eighteen million people *with no hope* in America alone. One can only imagine the number of hopeless souls worldwide. How sad. How tragic. If you've ever been there, you know how they feel. I certainly do.

It seems like everywhere I go, wherever people gather, there are stories of hopelessness when it comes to experiencing well-being at work. In conversing with people, I've found that many seem to have nowhere to turn. People are asking, "Where *do* I turn?" I've listened, I've absorbed, and I've learned. This book has been percolating in my mind for several years. I feel it's my obligation to share what I've learned.

If you are currently lost in the wilderness of joblessness, or if that wilderness is looming, take heart. When you're out of work, it can feel like you're all alone in that wilderness. Just know that you are not alone. Know that things can change in a moment with a phone call, an e-mail, a meeting with someone of influence, or a *book*.

Stand strong. Relief is on the way. In the meantime, beware. Beware of compounding your situation.

The Attraction of What We Don't Want

Worry does not empty tomorrow of its sorrow.
It empties today of its strength.
—Corrie ten Boom

When we start to lose hope, we tend to become buried under an avalanche of worry. It's cruel, but worry just compounds our problems.

Worry is the perfect storm for creating exactly what we don't want. It contains the perfect ingredients. Worry is a combination of *vibrant visualization* backed by *intense feeling*. We *feel* as we would if the object of our worry actually happened. We *feel* it in our gut.

Vibrant visualization + Intense feeling = Manifestation

People often say, "What I've feared the most has happened." Eliminate worry. If it creeps in, dismiss it.

We are going to take the above equation and make it work for us in positive ways. We need to change the visualization. The feelings part of the equation shown above is key.

Negative Feelings…Forever Gone!

It's the negative *feelings* that get you. Thoughts themselves don't hurt you. It's dwelling on the negative ones and their accompanying feelings that hurts. Plus, to make things worse, the *subsequent manifestation* that follows vivid, negative thoughts intensifies the hurt. Focusing on and accepting a thought as *true* leads to its associated feeling(s). Maybe you've had despairing thoughts like:

- How did I end up like this?
- How did all this happen to me?
- Why haven't things worked out?
- How could he or she do this to me?
- I am so alone.
- This "hole" is so deep I see no way out.

And maybe you've experienced the following feelings that accompany those thoughts:

- a sick feeling in the pit of the stomach
- melancholy
- despondency
- depression
- mourning
- sadness
- hopelessness

Dismiss them! They are a thing of the past. When negativity creeps in, dismiss it. Actually say out loud: "Dismissed!" Sweep the negative thought away. Replace it with the opposite positive thought. You'll feel better immediately, and you'll attract the positive. It's worked for me for years.

Situations Are Neutral

Remember that situations, conditions, events, and circumstances just *are what they are.* They are only *happenings.* They are *things*—and most of them are neutral. It's how we *react* to them, how we think and feel about them, that shapes our lives and determines our happiness. The exceptions are triumph and tragedy. When a triumph occurs, *absorb* it with every fiber of your being. Likewise, when a tragedy occurs, *endure* it with every fiber of your being. Ask yourself, "What *good* can I do as a result of this?"

Don't Lose Hope

One night many years ago, a traveling gentleman had to sleep in his car because he couldn't afford a one-night stay in a hotel. Five years later, Harry S. Truman became president of the United States.

Just because you might be down now doesn't mean you'll stay there. You *can* initiate change.

Have Faith

The past does not equal the future.
—Tony Robbins

Have faith. Have faith in faith. Faith feels good. Faith is believing in something before it makes its appearance. Faith precedes demonstration. Dig your ditches. In a drought, prepare for the coming rain. *Feel* as though what you desire has already manifested.

If you've been traveling down a wrong path in life, turn around right now. Start the process of a miraculous turnaround!

Don't let circumstances control your life. Take control of your life.

Right now means, this is where you are right now. It doesn't mean that this is where you're going to be tomorrow. It's time to move forward, starting right now!

A champion is someone who gets up when they can't.
—Jack Dempsey

CHAPTER SUMMARY

- The absence of well-being at work caused by a lack of good, satisfying work

- Constant, rapid change

- Implications

- Implications are often overwhelming

- Lost hope

- Don't lose hope

- Have faith

CALL TO ACTION

1. Understand and acknowledge that a lack of well-being at work is temporary.

2. Absorb the lessons in this book from this point forward.

3. Visit www.MPimpact.com to follow and contribute to our blog for inspiration.

Chapter 2

A Solution

Everything is energy, and that's all there is to it.
Match the frequency of the reality you want,
and you cannot help but get that reality.
It can be no other way. This is not philosophy. It is physics.
—Albert Einstein

There is a solution. *The Actions of Well-Being at Work* that are covered in this book will help you get to where you want to go. So hang in there. You must maintain a *can-do* mind-set. Any kind of attitude that goes against a can-do mind-set will get in the way of success.

Whoever you happen to be,
whatever work situation you are experiencing right now,

wherever you are in the world,

whether you are a white-collar worker or a blue-collar worker,

whether you work for or aspire to work for yourself or are a full-time
employee,

whether you are wandering in that occupational wilderness without
direction,

…there is hope.

Three Primary Motivators

Why do you have the *aspirations* you have? Why do you *do* what
you do? Why do you *want* what you want? Why do you *buy* what
you buy? Why do you *buy into* certain ideas and ideals? You and
everyone else do things, buy things, and buy into things for one
of, or any combination of, three reasons. Listed in order of *urgency*,
people desire to

1. relieve existing pain;
2. avoid potential pain;
3. achieve gain.

These are the three primary motivators behind everything we do.

What is the *consequence* of *not* addressing the urgency related to any
one of these areas? It is a living experience that falls short of well-being.

What is Your Primary Motivator?

Regarding motivation, where are you right now when it comes to
being gainfully employed? What does today look like for you?

*   Are you happily, gainfully employed, and do you want to stay
    that way?

- Are you concerned about job security? Is change lurking?
- Are you currently unemployed and looking for work?
- Are you currently employed and looking for better work?
- Are you mired in a job that is beneath your education and abilities?

Where is your urgency right now? Start from where you are, from what your reality is right now.

What *Must* Be Done

"Good enough" used to be good enough. But that's not true anymore. Starting right now, you must do everything you can do to *increase the likelihood* of maximizing and maintaining your value in the global workforce. Position yourself for ongoing, rewarding employment. Give yourself every advantage to find, keep, and prosper in good, satisfying work.

So what is the benefit for you?

The Benefit of Taking Action— What's In It For You?

Simply put, you can have well-being at work. There is nothing quite like the feeling of getting paid after delivering good, solid work. Maintaining good, satisfying work is a key ingredient to overall well-being. When you get paid for a job well done, *everything* is better.

Imagine

Imagine how it would feel—stop and truly imagine it—to experience consistent, lasting well-being at work. Many people are not experiencing anything close to that. Envision getting up in the morning and feeling really good about going to work every day. Visualize filling your days with purposeful and interesting activities.

Having good, meaningful work goes a long way toward your ability to experience overall well-being. When we do good, meaningful work, everything just feels better. We feel better about ourselves. We feel valuable. We feel successful, because we are.

There is also nothing quite like the feeling of getting paid after delivering good, solid work. Experiencing this consistently throughout your working years is an even better feeling. Maintaining good, satisfying work means keeping an income flowing. It is getting paid for a job well done.

Everything is better.

During the summers of my high school years, I worked as a helper for my father and uncle in their carpentry business. I remember receiving my first paycheck after my first week of work. It was for fifty dollars, but it was the most satisfying pay I have ever received. That money truly did bring with it a feeling that I'd never experienced before and haven't since. I distinctly remember how I felt when I went out and bought Paul and Linda McCartney's new album *Ram* with my freshly earned dollars. Bliss! I've been an avid collector of music all my life, but I've never enjoyed a first listen more than I did that one. The album was truly *mine*. I'd *earned* it.

Throughout the years I have experienced consistent income, but I have also suffered extended periods of time with little or no money coming in. I'll tell you something: both experiences are polar opposites when it comes to feelings.

If we are working, all facets of life feel better. Likewise, if we are not working, much about life can feel negative.

Overall Well-Being

How do you get more out of your personal life? Get the *most* out of your work life.

Overall well-being might mean different things for each of us. It's probably safe to say that no matter who you are or where you live in the world, overall well-being likely includes some or all of the following:

Love

- for your creator
- for others
- for yourself

A healthy

- spirit
- mind
- body

Financial stability and security

- income
- investment strategy
- home

How many of these desires can be directly or indirectly influenced by your ability to maintain gainful employment? I'm guessing that your answer is, "quite a few." I surely am not qualified to give advice on these specific areas. However, by applying the principles in this book, you can't help but have a positive impact on your overall well-being.

CHAPTER SUMMARY

- There is hope

- There is a solution. *The Actions of Well-Being at Work* that are discussed in this book

- The three primary motivators

- Imagine how it can be

- Well-being at work has an impact on your overall well-being

CALL TO ACTION

1. Read chapters 3 through 8. Absorb the knowledge and take the actions that will contribute to you experiencing well-being at work.

2. Visit www.MPimpact.com to follow and contribute to our blog.

PART 2

Chapter 3

You Enterprises

Strive not to be a success, but rather to be of value.

—Albert Einstein

L et's recognize once and for all that we all work for ourselves. We are all in our own business. From now on, when someone asks, "Whom do you work for?" I implore you to answer, "I work for my family and myself. I am employed by [insert name of your employer]."

This is the mind-set you must have. You *are* in business for yourself and your family. You are the Chief Executive Officer of your own enterprise. Your employer is your *customer*. Your employer pays you for a valuable service you provide that is related to customer service (whether your customer is internal or external). If the service you offer loses its value, you lose too.

The employer-employee relationship is tenuous. Things can change in a heartbeat. So you need to be prepared for change. You can never take the employer-employee relationship for granted.

Your employer does *not* owe you a living. Never forget this. You are not paid for your time; rather, you are paid for the value you provide during the time you work. Your employer exchanges his or her money for your value. So you need to be of value. Furthermore, as time goes on, you must continue to offer value, and you need to be of increasing value. What's more, you must be able to prove and validate your value.

The Value You Offer

What value *do* you offer? What admirable qualities do you possess? What might be unique about the value you offer? Unique value can be a very strong selling point in your bid to find and keep good, satisfying work. If you can't think of what unique value you possess, think harder. Everyone has his or her own one-of-a-kind story. Your particular story brought you to this point in your life. What did you learn along the way? What unusual skills or attributes have you acquired that are not very common?

Are you still not coming up with anything? Think about what distinctive skills would be valuable in your current or potential area of expertise. Then, work on acquiring those particular skills or attributes.

Make a list of the valuable qualities you can offer. Then turn the list into a value statement starting with, "The value I provide is…" This is your brand statement. Keep it at the ready. You will use it often.

Write it. Remember it. Speak it. *Live* it!

Be Invaluable

If you want to succeed at any job, make yourself invaluable.
Go the extra mile; make them never be able to imagine
what life without you there would be like.
—Ross Mathews

Deliver stellar performance. Offer ever-increasing value. Be a multi-faceted performer. Be like a human multifaceted tool. Aspire to be the world's best at whatever you do. Be *the* go-to person in your area of expertise.

Take the case of George Toma, a landscaper. His name came into national prominence thirty or so years before I began writing this book. I still remember his name. He was *the* expert when it came to preparing professional sports fields for playability. Who had ever heard of a landscaper of national prominence before George Toma? As the example of George shows, you can take anything, any profession, and turn yourself into *the* go-to expert if that is your aspiration.

Wayne Turmel, former stand-up comedian and former director of training, became the world-recognized, authority in the area of virtual presentations and meetings. I know Wayne personally. It was his combination of extensive learning, disciplined follow-through, and focused performance that earned him the distinction of being *the* expert in his field.

Be Visible

Stay "in front" of people. Stay visible. Stay invaluable. A great way to do this is by continuously writing. Through contributing to blogs and forums, you will become a recognized expert. Then, when the time comes to make a change, you will have generated a network of people who know you and the value you offer. By writing, you will be actively preparing to stay gainfully employed! Do you think the authority in any profession would ever have trouble getting a job? It is highly unlikely—*if* that expert remained current within a viable industry. So if you aspire to be a specialist in a particular profession, then go for it! Hey, why not? Someone has to be number one. Why not you?

Add Some Invaluable Value— Inspire, Enable, and Encourage Others

Inspire   with your *actions*

Enable   with your *teaching, training, coaching,* and *mentoring*

Encourage   with your *words*

Have you ever noticed that the world is full of discouragers? People never seem to have a problem telling you why something won't work. In fact, there seems to be a multitude of "experts" who can tell you why something won't work. Instead, strive to be different. Be an *encourager* of people. Give them the courage to go for it! They'll love you for it. Not only that, they'll see you as invaluable.

Resources for Becoming Highly Valuable

On your journey to number one, you will acquire specialized knowledge from a variety of resources. *The Actions of Well-Being at Work* that this book discusses will give you the knowledge and skills to help you make the most of those resources and the opportunities they offer. Living *The Actions of Well-Being at Work* will keep you invaluable.

A Unique Approach to Finding Work

Several years ago, while I was looking for good, satisfying work, I tried a unique approach. I gave careful consideration to what potential employers *needed* in the way of value from a potential employee. I then considered how the value that I offered would satisfy those needs. I crafted a one-page document with the sections "You Need" and "I Offer" to indicate how I would meet the needs of employers. I decided to try this approach as opposed to sending a traditional cover letter and résumé. I mailed the document in an envelope to fifty potential employers in the industry I was looking to penetrate. I heard back from fourteen of those potential employers—an unheard of 27 percent return on a piece of direct mail! My tactic proved to be very effective. In fact, I established a lucrative relationship with one of those employers that continues to this day.

On the following page is the actual document I sent to those prospective employers. Following my document is a blank template you can use if you'd like to try the same approach. Keep in mind that I was looking for contract work as a freelance trainer/coach. If you are looking for full-time work, adjust your wording accordingly. Give it a try. It worked like a charm for me.

Garrett G. Terhune

(973)945-3622

gterhune@MPimpact.com

www.MPimpact.com

Performance Excellence Consultant

Perhaps I can be of service to you, your organization, and your clients. My name is Garrett Terhune. I am a corporate performance excellence consultant with extensive classroom/instructor-led and live online training and coaching experience. I successfully conduct *presentation skills, sales, technology/software, and train-the-trainer* training, coaching, and consulting for some of the world's most prestigious corporations. The purpose of this correspondence is to offer my services as a **per diem, per project, contract training resource**.

When the need for *optimal* training assistance arises…

You Need	I Offer
Maximum Positive Impact* and Action	Training focused on what the student *needs* to know and delivered with energy, conviction, and enthusiasm. Presented in a way that promises *Maximum Positive Impact®* with a clear message that's understood and that promotes on-the-job action.
Results	The ability to communicate effectively and to explain sometimes complex material in a clear, concise, and easy-to-understand manner that directly results in student success. Clearly understood training that focuses on *practical on-the-job application* versus theoretical classroom elegance.
Experience, Dedication, and Professionalism	30+ years of professional training, coaching, and consulting experience. Motivating and coaching my students in a firm, encouraging, and enthusiastic manner are among my major strengths.
Reliability	Dependability. When it's "game time," I'm there—prepared, rehearsed, and organized with a clear understanding of the student's needs.

Please contact me when the need for an accomplished trainer or coach presents itself.

I'll be happy to provide my résumé and references upon request. Rate requirements are flexible, depending on the scope of the opportunity.

Your Name
Your Phone Number
Your E-mail Address
Your Website

Your Title

One-paragraph description of what you do and what you propose

When the need for *optimal* _____ arises…

You Need	**I Offer**
Major Employer Need #1	A one-paragraph description about how you satisfy need #1.
Major Employer Need #2	A one-paragraph description about how you satisfy need #2
Major Employer Need #3	A one-paragraph description about how you satisfy need #3
Major Employer Need #4	A one-paragraph description about how you satisfy need #4

Please contact me when the need for an accomplished _____ presents itself.

I'll be happy to provide my résumé and references upon request.

(Add a short statement regarding your rate requirements. You can list specific rates or leave it open for discussion.)

I look forward to hearing from you.

Goals

People with goals succeed because they know where they're going.
—Earl Nightingale

Before you can be where you want to be, you have to know where you want to go. George Harrison sang, "If you don't know where you're going, any road will take you there." How true.

What *is* your goal? Where *do* you want to be?

When it comes to well-being at work, do you currently have a direction? If you are not employed or are not happy in your current occupation, do you offer employable value? If not, this is your first order of business. What career/occupation will you pursue? In what industries are there high areas of need? In what areas do you already possess some aptitude or experience? What *will* you pursue in terms of acquiring marketable knowledge and skills? Where and how will you acquire such knowledge and skills? All of these are good questions to consider.

Once you decide on your occupational goal and the value you must possess to reach that goal, the first two *Actions of Well-Being at Work* will serve as vehicles to accelerate the process.

If you already possess marketable value, are employed, and are happy in your current occupation, how will you stay progressive and on the cutting edge? What goal will you set for expanding your current value? How will you stay highly marketable for the time when change comes?

To help reach your goals, use the following goal-achieving formula and get some help from the four "mentors."

The Maximum Positive Impact
Goal-Achieving Formula

1. Where do I want to be (regarding my goal)? (Figure out *exactly* what you want. Be very specific.) *My specific goal is*_____. I will achieve my goal by _____.

2. Where am I *currently* (regarding my goal)?

3. What are *potential challenges* to getting to where I want to be? Why am I not there now?

4. *Why* do I want to be there? What is my *motivation*? What is the *benefit* for me?

5. Am I primarily looking to *relieve existing pain*, *avoid potential pain*, or *achieve gain*? On a scale of one to ten, how high is my level of urgency to reach my goal? (Without urgency, change is unlikely.)

6. What *help* do I need?

7. Do I have the *means* to get there? If not, how can I *acquire* the means? What *means/resource(s)* do I need? *Who* can help me?

8. What have I *tried* in the past that didn't work? *Why* didn't it work? What did I *learn* from those experiences?

9. Which aspects of what I tried in the past *did* work? How can I *leverage* those successes?

Figure 3.1

D.D.F.M—Your Four Goal-Achieving Mentors

To help you achieve your goal, use the following four "mentors."

1. *Determination.* Be determined to succeed. Have the attitude that nothing will stop you. A determined person is hard to stop.

2. *Discipline.* Be disciplined in pursuing your goal. Be disciplined in taking the specific actions that will get you there, and then *take* those actions.

3. *Focus.* Focus on the action of the moment. Be intensely focused on the task at hand. Eliminate potential distractions.

4. *Measurement.** Measure your progress.
   - How will you measure progress?
   - What will you use to measure your progress?
   - What do successful steps look like?

*To help you measure your progress in implementing *The Actions of Well-Being at Work* you'll read about later in this book, I've provided various measurement tools. You'll find these tools near the end of each lesson. By going to Appendix A, you can order your free working electronic versions of these tools.

All-Consuming

To really bring the goal home, if there is true urgency, make your goal *all-consuming*. With "*it*" being your goal, proceed as follows:

- Dwell on *it*.
- Be all-consumed with *it*.

- Always keep *it* in front of you.
- Don't let *it* out of sight or out of mind.
- If *it* is not constantly in front of you, *it* will lose steam.*
- Drift off to sleep dwelling on *its* manifestation.
- Awaken to feelings of *its* manifestation.
- Be obsessed with completing the tasks necessary to realize *its* manifestation.
- Be obsessed with *its* realization.
- Dwell on the feelings that are accompanied by *its* success.

* As a constant reminder to focus on an urgent goal, I keep a teakettle on my desk. I'm looking at it as I type this sentence. It is a constant reminder to keep my all-consuming goal on the front burner or it will lose steam. We know what happens to momentum when we say, "I'm going to put it on the back burner."

The Bank of Well-Being

Every day, make a deposit into your bank of well-being. Make sure to deposit

- every effort;
- every success;
- every trial and error (which moves you a step closer to success);
- every new thing you learn; and
- everything you do…

that maximizes and maintains your value in the global workforce.

Be patient. With consistency, and over time, your account will be overflowing with well-being.

When a Setback or Disappointment Occurs (and It Will)

Be resilient:

1. Deal with it.
2. Get over it.
3. Get on with it.

Move *forward* ➲ *Keep moving forward!*

Keep your eye on the prize.

In one of my all-time favorite books, Garth Stein's *The Art of Racing in the Rain* (which is, incidentally, a story told by a dog), the dog's owner, Denny, is a race car driver. Throughout the book, Denny repeatedly says, "The car goes where the eyes go." These are words of wisdom for pursuing any goal.

Now, I want to note one more thing about running "You Enterprises."

The Language of Finance

Become an expert in your personal finances. Finance is well beyond the scope of this book, so go to the vast resources out there and learn. The expertise will serve you well. Being the Chief Executive Officer of You Enterprises requires you to pay attention to your business's finances. You are also the Chief Financial Officer of You Enterprises. Learn to speak the language of finance. Understand and use the power of compound interest. Consistency over time wins.

People who say money isn't everything tend to be those who have money. Money has a great impact on well-being. Learn about money. Invest wisely. Become an expert in your finances.

Action!

Action may not bring happiness,
but there is no happiness without action.
—William James

Information – Action = 0

History did not happen in the past. History happened in the moment. *Every* history-making event happened in the moment. A *history* of excellence happened over many individual moments.

Every day, build *your* history of excellence. History happens *today*! How will *you* make history today? Your history of well-being at work starts right now. Do not procrastinate. *Do it now!*

Make today your masterpiece.
—Joshua Wooden

A Special Message to Young People

You possess a once-in-a-lifetime opportunity. It's called youth. Perform today's tasks superbly. Consistency over time wins. Enjoy the journey. Put away a percentage of your income starting now, and do it forevermore. Let compound interest do its thing.

Also, let compound learning do its thing.

Build a history of excellence. You've got the blessing of time on your side.

CHAPTER SUMMARY

- You are the Chief Executive Officer of You Enterprises.

- Your employer is your customer.

- What value do you currently offer?

- Be invaluable.

- Pursue your goals.

- Use the Maximum Positive Impact Goal-Achieving Formula.

- Take advantage of the "mentors" of determination, discipline, focus, and measurement to help you achieve your goals.

- Continuously make deposits in your "bank" of well-being.

- Be resilient.

- Take action! Information – Action = 0.

CALL TO ACTION

1. Go to Appendix A of this book and order your free copy of the **Well-Being at Work Toolkit**.

2. Print, in color, the **Well-Being at Work Quick Reference Card**. Have it laminated at your local office supply store. Keep it visible to help you stay on track.

Plus…

3. Use this book as a catalyst for achieving your goals.

4. Take on the mind-set that your job or upcoming job is your own business: You Enterprises.

5. Take on the mind-set that your employer or future employer is your customer.

6. Make a list of the value you offer (and continuously add to this list).

7. Using the list of the value you offer, create your value statement. Begin by saying, "The value I provide is…" This becomes your brand statement.

8. Memorize your brand statement.

9. Set your goal(s).

10. Take action!

11. Visit www.MPimpact.com to follow and contribute to our blog.

SURVEY

Will I implement the call to action above?

a) Yes! Right now.

b) Yes! But I'm so busy at the moment. I'll do it as soon as I have the chance.

c) Hmm…things are good right now. The urgency isn't there. But I know change lurks.

REFLECTION

To *embed* the knowledge and skills just learned, answer the following questions.

1. *What* did I learn?
   - How can I apply this knowledge to my work?

   - How will it make me more efficient?

   - How can this information help me provide better customer service?

   - How can this insight make me more valuable?

2. *How, when,* and *where* can I *follow through* to stay progressive and maintain these skills? (Practice in my attempt to perfect them.)

3. *How, when,* and *where* can I *apply* the knowledge I acquired and *perform* the skills I have learned?

Chapter 4

The Maximum Positive Impact
Pillars of Well-Being at Work

1. The Hierarchy of Well-Being at Work

2. The Actions of Well-Being at Work

3. The Cycle of Excellence

4. The Power Unit

5. The Customer

The Pillars

How can you stay strong when adversity strikes? How can you remain on the straight and narrow even when change blindsides you? You need something to support you. You need pillars of strength on which you can rely.

These pillars will hold you up when you feel the world is conspiring to take you down. You can depend on the pillars. They will always be there. Organizations may come and go. Teachers *will* come and go. Coaches *might* come and go. But you can count on the pillars to always be there for you.

These days, we just can't seem to grasp on to anything that will last. As soon as we do grab hold of something or come close to grabbing it, it goes away or changes. As soon as we get comfortable with technology, it changes. As soon as we get comfortable with our jobs, something changes. Pillars, though, stand the test of time.

This book is pillar based. Over the next several pages, I introduce you to each pillar. Throughout this book, you will see these pillars popping up in all that you do.

Rely on these pillars.

PILLAR 1

The Hierarchy of Well-Being at Work

Well-Being at Work

∩

Employability

Maintain relevant value

∩

Experience

Performance over time

∩

Fine-Tuning

of your preparation and performance

∩

Assessment

of your preparation and performance

∩

Performance

Apply specialized knowledge and skills
"Consistent, high-quality, on-the-job performance"

∩

Preparation

Practice/prepare thoroughly to perform

∩

Follow Through

Progress and maintain specialized knowledge and skills

∩

Learning
Attain specialized knowledge and skills
"Learning precedes performance"

☊

Focus, Determination, and Discipline
Be determined to succeed and DO what it takes!

☊

Decision
Make the decision to actively pursue your desire—decide on the
path to take

☊

Desire
For a good, fulfilling, happy life
"Overall Well-Being"

This is your path to well-being at work. Each step along the way carries with it a responsibility for you to thoroughly complete the step and then move forward. This path will put you in a terrific position to enjoy the numerous benefits of well-being at work.

Let's take a closer look at each step from the bottom up.

Desire. It must start here. You must care enough about where you want to go before you begin your journey. If this burning desire isn't present, it is unlikely you'll have the staying power to achieve the well-being at work that greatly contributes to overall well-being.

Decision. The decision must be "yes," as in, "Yes, I commit to actively pursuing my desire for well-being at work." It is here that you must decide which path to take. What occupation will you pursue? Will you take a new and different path, or do you want to rededicate yourself to a path you've already started on? Make the decision, and make the commitment to follow the path.

Focus, Determination, and Discipline. Without all three of these, success is unlikely. Focus on the task or responsibility at hand. Block out all distractions. You must be *determined* to get what you want. A determined person is hard to stop. You must also be disciplined— disciplined to do what must be done even if you don't feel like doing it. Even if it is uncomfortable, do it anyway!

> *We must all suffer one of two things:*
> *the pain of discipline or the pain of regret or disappointment.*
> —Jim Rohn

Learning. This is the point at which, based on your decision, you will start attaining the specialized knowledge and skills you'll need to perform. This is the beginning of your journey to subject-matter-expert status. (Action 1—"How to Learn with Maximum Positive Impact" will be covered in Chapter 5.)

Follow Through. Stay progressive. You must have discipline and stay current with your knowledge and skills. Change is constant and rapid in our world today. So it is imperative that you stay on the cutting edge. It's also important to get help. As you will see in the coming pages that discuss the Power Unit, you will not be going it alone. There truly is power in numbers. (Action 2—"How to Follow Through with Maximum Positive Impact" will be covered in Chapter 6.)

Preparation. Albert Einstein said, "The only source of knowledge is experience." You get experience by *doing*. So keep honing your skills.

Keep honing your expertise. Doctors and lawyers call their businesses "practices" for a reason. It is all about perpetually practicing. As they say, practice does not make perfect—perfect practice makes perfect.

Performance. It's show time! And perform you must. Anything less than stellar performance is just potential. Potential means that nothing important has been done yet. Stellar performers get employed. Stellar performers *stay* employed. (Action 3—"How to Perform with Maximum Positive Impact" will be covered in Chapter 7.)

Assessment. Don't wait for performance reviews. Instead, assess yourself after each preparation and performance. Be more scrupulous in your self-assessment than your boss will ever be. On a scale of one to ten, rate yourself on key aspects of your preparation and performance. (Assessment Tools to help you self-assess appear at the end of each "Action" chapter.)

Fine-Tuning. Based on your assessment, what can you do better next time? Even tiny improvements will grow to be big differentiators in your performance. Your capabilities will improve, and your value will increase exponentially. (Fine-Tuning Tools are available to help you fine-tune at the end of each "Action" chapter.)

Experience. Incorporating a thorough combination of everything discussed above will lead to a wealth of experience over time. This is something you can't accelerate. Time moves at its own pace. You'll get there! Be patient. Just focus on the task at hand.

Employability. When you maintain relevant value, you make sure you are always on the cutting edge. This keeps you in a position of being a sought-after talent. Become employable and stay that way.

When things change—and you know they will—you will need to go out and market yourself.

Well-Being at Work. This is your desired outcome!

PILLAR 2

The Actions of Well-Being at Work

Performance

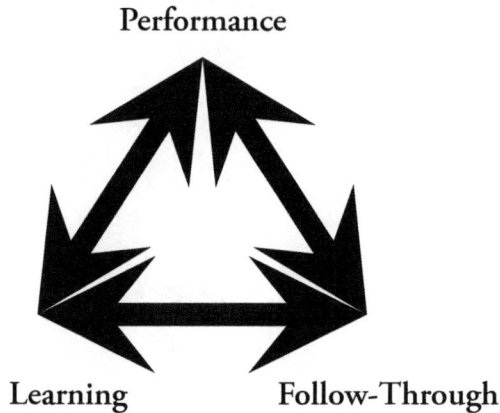

Learning   Follow-Through

The Actions of Well-Being at Work, as depicted above, are

1. performance;
2. continuous learning; and
3. consistent, disciplined, progressive follow-through.

These actions will help you

- *find* good, satisfying work;
- *keep* good, satisfying work;
- *find better*, satisfying work; and
- stay *employable.*

If you've ever wondered what you can do to accomplish any of the above outcomes, these are specific actions you can take. These are three things you can do.

Performance. This is about doing, about being productive. You must perform your on-the-job tasks. Perform and complete all the responsibilities related to your work. Apply your "stuff." Put your expertise to work. Use your knowledge and skills on the job. This is the result of learning and follow-through.

Learning. You must acquire knowledge and skills. Learn what you need to *know* and *do* to successfully execute your work. Make sure you really *know*. Continuously learn in your chosen area of expertise. This is a means to the desired end: performance.

Follow-Through. Maintain and enhance the knowledge and skills you have learned. Progress. This involves self-study and research, practice, and the receiving of coaching. Keep your knowledge and skills on the cutting edge. This is a means to the desired end: performance.

Learning + Follow-through =
The Foundation of Performance

Each action in the diagram supports the other. The two-way arrows represent the interconnectivity between each action in the strategy.

PILLAR 3

The Cycle of Excellence

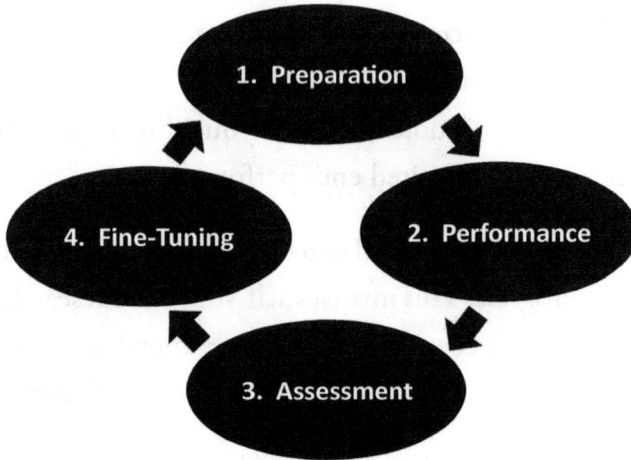

This is the model that will carry you to *performance excellence*. You will be inspecting your own efforts, because when it comes to your own well-being, no one has more at stake than you do. Each step in this model needs to be thoroughly completed to assure performance excellence and the well-being that accompanies it.

1. Preparation

Maximum Positive Impact *preparation* encompasses every essential thing you can do before engaging in any of the three actions outlined in *The Actions of Well-Being at Work*. To recap, the actions are as follows.

- **Learning**—receiving training
- **Follow-Through**—includes engaging in a coaching session to help assure your success
- **Performance**—performing your work

Thorough preparation before taking an action increases the likelihood of a richer, more successful experience during the action event.

2. Performance

Maximum Positive Impact *performance* is you performing during the action. It means you actively taking part during a learning event. It means you actively participating during follow-through coaching. It means you *doing* your everyday, on-the-job tasks.

3. Assessment

Maximum Positive Impact *assessment* is about you assessing both your preparation before an action event and your performance during an action event.

4. Fine-Tuning

Maximum Positive Impact *fine-tuning* is you analyzing your assessment and then doing what needs to be done to improve both preparation and performance for the very next action event that will occur (and all subsequent events thereafter). In other words, it is about continuous improvement.

PILLAR 4

The Power Unit
(*The Power of Three*)

You, the Performer
You, the learner
You, the coachee

Communication

Learning Provider   **Coach/Mentor**
—Face-to-face-instructor led
—Virtual-instructor led
—Computer based, self-paced

This is the support unit that will keep you performing. There truly is power in numbers. Don't go it alone. Secure your support foundation.

Introducing the Power Unit—the Power of Three

These magical entities are as follows:

- **You, the performer**. As the performer, you have several functions in the Power Unit: (1) you are the learner; (2) you follow through, and you are the coachee; and (3) you are the on-the-job performer. You are the constant presence within the Power Unit.

- **The learning provider**. These entities provide you with essential knowledge and skills. Learning providers come in several "flavors": trainers, facilitators, teachers, professors, consultants, colleagues, bosses, self-paced online programs, live online programs, books, seminars, workshops, and more. Learning providers come and go.

- **The coach/mentor**. These individuals keep you performing with excellence. A coach might last for a project, throughout your tenure with the employer, or even for a lifetime. A mentor might be a living individual or someone you've never met. A mentor might be someone you deeply admire from the past. A mentor might be a historical figure.

So, yes, the individuals associated with your Power Unit are ever changing. They are dynamic. You might have, and probably will have, several learning providers all at once. You might have more than one coach, depending on the project or particular task. The only constant is you. What's important is that the roles of Learning Provider and Coach/Mentor *always* remain filled. The power of three—it's a powerful combination.

Three work together to support *you*. Three work together to assure *your* performance is on the cutting edge. There is courage in numbers. Three (the Power Unit) versus one (you going it alone) is powerful. It means the odds of succeeding are with you. Become a *powerful* unit of three. Alone, you can become vulnerable. Alone, you can fall back on bad habits. Alone, you can become satisfied with your performance *just as it is.*

You, the individual—you, the performer—are paramount. But now you are supported by a concrete foundation of effective learning providers and coaches. You must be actively involved in your own development. There must be ongoing communication between the three key entities.

The foundation of performance excellence
begins with effective learning.
It *continues* with effective follow-through and coaching.

This strategy encourages the three key roles—Performer, Learning Provider, and Coach/Mentor—to work in unison. Each member of this powerful team knows exactly what to expect from the others. Each member truly understands the perspectives of the others. Each holds the others accountable. This three-role Power Unit enables exemplary performance that lone individuals typically cannot achieve.

The *communication* between the three roles must be crystal clear, open, and trusting.

When each of these key roles performs with maximum positive impact it *significantly increases the likelihood of greater individual and organizational success.* It's about people supporting people. Chances are that you will also be an active participant in a Power Unit of other performers. You will be a learning provider for other performers. You will be the coach/mentor for other performers. Power Units enable powerful performance.

PILLAR 5

The Customer

Customers are your most valuable asset. They are your employer's most valuable asset. Customers are the most valuable asset to your well-being at work. Customers determine whether you keep working or not. You are always at the mercy of your customer. And you serve two customers:

1. those who purchase your employer's products or services (the customers who exchange their money for products or services provided by your employer)
2. your employer (yes, your employer is your customer)

Your boss is your customer's representative. Your boss is the liaison between you and the customer organization (your employer).

The customer keeps you gainfully employed. The customer leads to others becoming gainfully employed. Customers generate revenue. Revenue keeps businesses in business. Successful, revenue-generating businesses keep people employed and employ more people.

When it comes to customers, beware of becoming indifferent. Beware of not giving your customer your full, undivided attention. When customers make their appearance, whether face-to-face or through other communication, that means, stop everything! *The customer must now become the focus of your complete attention.*

You might get by with indifference as far as your employer is concerned—for a while. Employers must comply with laws and policy regarding termination. But you will *not* get by with your customers. Why? Because your indifference will affect their business and their livelihood. They don't have the time or patience for someone who doesn't have their best interest in mind. Customers can fire you in an instant…and they will. You'll be gone quicker than a spring snow. That might sound like a cruel statement, but I want it to hit home. It's reality.

Customers keep you gainfully employed.

Next we will get to the heart of your well-being at work becoming and remaining a reality—*The Actions of Well-Being at Work.*

CHAPTER SUMMARY

- The Maximum Positive Impact *Pillars of Well-Being at Work*
  1. The Hierarchy of Well-Being at Work
  2. The Actions of Well-Being at Work
  3. The Cycle of Excellence
  4. The Power Unit (*The Power of Three*)
  5. The Customer

- You can rely on these pillars. They are the foundation of well-being at work.

- Lean on your Power Unit. Don't go it alone. There is strength in numbers.

CALL TO ACTION

1. Refer often to these pillars.

2. Stay in touch with your learning providers.

3. Find a coach.

4. Find a mentor.

5. Treat customers like gold.

6. Visit www.MPimpact.com to follow and contribute to our blog.

PART 3

The Actions of Well-Being at Work

The only place success comes before work is in the dictionary.
—Vince Lombardi

We now delve into the *three concrete actions* you can take to achieve well-being at work. Without all three, you are unlikely to achieve lasting success at work.

The subtitle of this book references "Maximizing Your Value." *The Actions of Well-Being at Work* provide the guidelines for maximizing your value. The three concrete actions include

1. learning…how to perform;
2. following through…to stay current and cutting-edge; and
3. performing…like the world-class on-the-job performer you need to be.

All three actions are your *path to mastery*.

Coming up are the guidelines for each action. Throughout these lessons, we'll start incorporating the *Pillars of Well-Being at Work* in force.

Within each action, you'll find step-by-step procedures for each stage of the *Cycle of Excellence*. The Cycle of Excellence will guide you through each action, and it will become clear how to use the cycle as we move forward. Every step will increase the likelihood of you getting the most from your time and efforts.

These actions come from my firsthand experience. I know they work. These actions have led me to enjoy the successes I've had in my career.

Let's start with the first step leading to your own well-being at work.

Chapter 5

Action 1: How to *Learn* with Maximum Positive Impact

*The first and most important ability you can develop
in the flat world is the ability to "learn how to learn"—
to constantly absorb, and teach yourself new ways of doing
old things or new ways of doing new things.*
—Thomas L. Friedman

Learning

Learning may be defined as the attainment of specialized knowledge or skills. It is the start of your path to mastery. It is the first step to securing marketable subject-matter expertise. Possessing this kind of competence is paramount to finding and keeping rewarding employment.

71

Learning enables performance. Unacceptable or *less-than-standard* performance will greatly hinder your ability to stay employed. Of course, you might say, everyone knows that. But there is a difference between knowing something and actually doing something about it. The first part of doing something about it is to be aware of a potential problem. This potential problem *must* be addressed.

For virtually every company, the scarce resource today is human ability.
—Geoff Colvin, *Talent Is Overrated*

A Potential Problem—The Downward Spiral

I believe the root cause of unacceptable or less-than-standard performance is all too often *ineffective training and coaching.*

The fact is that all learning opportunities are not equally effective. This means that everyone is not receiving an equal opportunity to *learn.* Therefore, everyone is not getting an equal opportunity to *perform.*

Less-than-excellent performance leads to employees negatively affecting customer service, which leads to waning customer acquisition and fewer customers retained. This means fewer customers. Fewer customers affect an organization's profitability and success, which leads to a struggling organization, which means fewer or no jobs are being added, and many jobs are being subtracted.

The result is a global job shortage.

I can't begin to tell you about the inconsistencies I've personally witnessed over the years in learning-provider effectiveness. These inconsistencies are unacceptable. *This* problem *can* be solved—and *you* can solve it.

Maximum Positive Impact, Inc. and our well-being at work approach make ineffective training and coaching obsolete. You need to always ask yourself the question, how reliable and effective is the learning source I'm considering?

When it comes to learning, you have several avenues to choose from:
- face-to-face-instructor-led training
- virtual-instructor-led training
- video-instructor-led learning
- video self-paced learning
- self-paced electronic learning
- books
- experience
- _____ (other)

Regarding all of these avenues, a question most people don't ask but should is, how reliable and effective is the teaching source?

People attend a learning event and assume it will be led by a competent, knowledgeable instructor. We place our trust in the person at the front of the room or on the other end of the virtual tool. We assume that self-paced learning offerings will be effective learning vehicles. But if all learning *opportunities* or all learning *providers* are not equal in their effectiveness, are you willing to chance it? You might get an excellent, professional trainer, or you might not. Are you willing to put your livelihood in the hands of someone or into some program that will have a negative impact on your ability to perform?

The Cause

Why might you get less-than-excellent direction when it comes to acquiring the knowledge and skills you must have to make a good, satisfying living? If we are talking about instructor-led delivery, your instructors just might not be very good. They might lack subject-matter expertise. They might not have effective teaching ability. They might be strapped with poor material or a poorly written program. What if they are simply not very engaging? What if they are just going through the motions? What if they are just not having a good day and are not at their best? What if they just don't care very much? What if they're doing just enough to remain employed? There are lots of "what ifs," and it's not comforting when we think of it that way. Who loses? You do, in a big way.

I can tell you from personal experience that there is a *huge* gap in effectiveness from trainer to trainer. This inconsistency can deliver a crushing blow to your performance and therefore to your livelihood and well-being.

How Do *I* Know?

When it comes to all learning opportunities not being equally effective, I believe it might be a fifty-fifty proposition *at best*. How do I know? Over the years, I have had many opportunities to co-instruct in the same classroom with many instructors. I knew exactly what was supposed to be delivered. But I have witnessed *stunning* incompetency firsthand. It happens more often than one would think. I have worked with instructors who had great reputations, but I was shocked when I witnessed their performance. I wondered how many people over the years had been affected in a negative way by receiving poor training from these individuals. The sad part is that students don't even know what they're *not* getting. Shockingly, these instructors' post class evaluations are often good or even great because they were nice, funny, good-looking, and so on. So who knew?

Over-the-Shoulder Trainers

In these days of fewer people doing more and more, many employees are asked to train others. In other words, nonprofessional trainers are asked to stop doing their jobs in order to go teach someone else the ropes. In his excellent book *To Sell Is Human*, Daniel H. Pink states, "When I surveyed a group of people on how much time they spent teaching, coaching, or instructing others, nearly 37 percent of respondents said they devoted a *significant amount of time* to doing so." We should remember that these folks are probably doing the best they can under the circumstances.

After absorbing the competencies in this chapter, you will be able to help your trainers provide you with what you need to learn.

How *Do* You Know?

So how do you know? How do you know if the training provided to you is effective or ineffective. How do you know if the trainer is competent or incompetent? Yes, there are many excellent professional trainers and excellent online programs out there, but how *do* you know? How do you know who is leading your learning opportunity? If you are lucky enough to get a confident, caring, professional learning provider, then good for you. How do you know a certain online learning program is effective and will give you what you need? This can't be left to chance.

This chapter will give you checkpoints. It provides techniques and questions to ensure you are not shortchanged. You must be sure that what you're receiving gives you the best opportunity to perform. If you find that a learning provider is not delivering what's described in this chapter, you need to ask for what you're not getting. You must guide them to give you what you need.

The Implications of Ineffective Learning Providers

The implications of receiving less-than-accurate, less-than-effective learning can be catastrophic to your well-being at work. You are paid to perform. So if you don't know how to perform a particular task, or if you are performing it incorrectly, it will affect the value you offer.

- Your performance will suffer.
- Your morale will take a hit.
- Organizational performance will suffer.
- Customers will suffer.

Good enough used to be good enough, but not anymore. It doesn't matter if the training is live (face-to-face), virtual, computer based, self-paced, or based on video or some other platform—if you're not getting what you need, you're not getting what you need. Period. You must not be a victim. You must hold learning providers accountable.

You need to be proactive and *go get* what you need. Don't settle for less. You can't afford to. Too much is at stake. Your livelihood and well-being are at stake.

Understand what you should expect from learning providers.

Good News

The good news is that there is much that *you* can do to

1. hold the learning provider accountable;
2. increase the likelihood of successful learning;
3. ensure that the learning converts to consistent on-the-job performance excellence; and
4. maintain performance excellence.

Yes! Hold your learning providers accountable. Your occupational and overall well-being depend on it.

Let's learn!

S U R V E Y

I feel I always make the very most of my learning opportunities.
   a) True
   b) False

The Power Unit
(*The Power of Three*)

You, the Performer

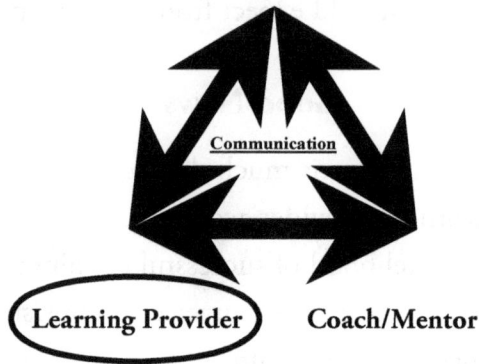

Learning Provider **Coach/Mentor**

The Learning Provider: One of the key functions of the Power Unit is the focus of this competency. Your function in this action is that of learner.

Learning Precedes Performance

For everything you can now *do*, you once had to learn how to do it. For everything you now *know*, you once had to acquire the knowledge. This knowledge and skill base that you possess seems like second nature. You don't have to think about it. You just know. You just know how to do it. That's great—for right now. But with the constant, rapid change that occurs in today's world, the knowledge and skills you possess today might be obsolete tomorrow. Therefore, you constantly need to retool yourself with updated knowledge and skills, or you'll get left behind. So learning is going to be a major part of your working life forevermore. You must maximize your learning opportunities.

78

This competency, "How to Learn with Maximum Positive Impact," is about doing everything you can to make your learning experience rich and rewarding. It's about gaining every advantage possible. It's about making sure you *truly learn*.

The Session Introduction

Note that I've separated these points out into nine distinct steps. Later in this chapter, when we get into The Session Introduction, this format will become clear to you. Seeing it laid out this way here will give you a clearer understanding of the concept.

1. **What is "How to *Learn* with Maximum Positive Impact"?**

   "How to *Learn* with Maximum Positive Impact" is a lesson focusing on what you can do *before*, *during*, and *after* a learning opportunity to maximize your learning and convert knowledge and skills into consistent on-the-job performance excellence. This competency provides the *processes*, *techniques*, and *tools* you need to apply these best practices when preparing for and participating in a learning opportunity.

2. **What is its purpose?**

   The lesson's purpose is to increase the likelihood of you, the performer, delivering sustainable, optimal on-the-job performance resulting from what you've learned. Not being optimally trained can have an impact on you, your department, your company, and your company's customers. Competition for your company's business and for your job is fierce. Everyone must be prepared to compete as never before.

3. **Why implement *this* approach?**

Nothing bad can happen by doing what this chapter is asking you to do. You must be responsible for your own development. You must be responsible for your own future. One of my favorite business philosophers, Jim Rohn, said, "If you don't design your own life plan, chances are you'll fall into someone else's plan. And guess what they may have planned for you? Not much."

4. **What are the implications of not acting now?**

You could potentially get left behind. You could potentially miss out on work because someone else may be more eager, prepared, and passionate about doing your kind of work.

5. **Why *this* particular approach?**

It focuses on practical, everyday usefulness, not on theoretical classroom elegance. It takes into account your workload. This approach is designed to blend in with your current responsibilities. It makes your life (in the role of performer) more effective.

6. **What is the evidence that the approach works?**

You can be the judge. I won't bury you under an avalanche of information. I just provide the essentials that drive the competencies' success.

7. **What's in it for you? (WIIFY)**

You can truly acquire knowledge and skills so that you can find and keep good, satisfying work.

8. **What are some examples of its practical application?**

The practices covered in this lesson will enable you to consistently learn with maximum positive impact. The practices will give you crystal-clear direction on how to make the most of every learning opportunity in which you participate from this point forward.

9. **What is the expected outcome?**

   By the end of this chapter, you will know how to maximize your learning so that you can perform with consistent excellence.

Regarding what you'll read throughout this lesson (and the next two lessons), keep in mind that your learning provider does *not* have to provide the information in the exact formats and in the exact order that I've presented them in. In fact, he or she probably won't. Unless learning providers have been trained by Maximum Positive Impact, Inc., it is highly unlikely they will deliver this information in the sequence in which you'll see it in these pages. The sequence is not important. What *is* important is making sure that you get all of the vital information.

The labels or names I've given to the "boxes of information" are aimed at helping you separate the information into understandable segments.

Just know that the formats provided help you

- experience learning in a way that will maximize the effectiveness of the learning event;
- maximize the likelihood of thoroughly understanding the content delivered; and
- know what and how content should be delivered and what you should be receiving.

Understanding how a learning provider "unwraps" a new topic or skill will go a long way toward helping you comprehend it. Experiencing learning in this way makes it as complete a learning experience as possible. It increases your likelihood of "getting it."

Be alert, and keep your eyes and ears open for this information. If you're not receiving it, *ask for it.*

SURVEY

This best describes me when I participate in a learning program:
- a) I am more interested in getting out of class than getting something out of class.
- b) I am thinking about all the work I could be doing.
- c) I actively participate and try to make the most of the learning opportunity.

How to *Learn* with Maximum Positive Impact

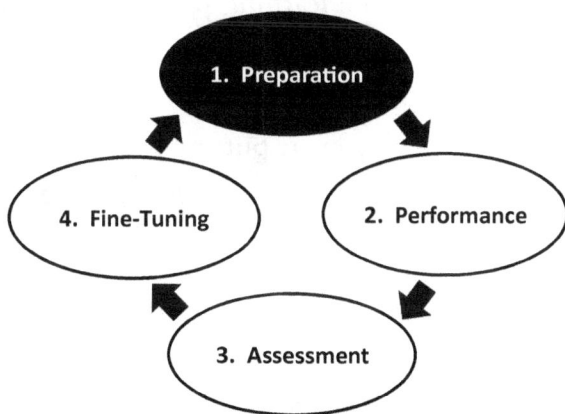

```
                    ┌─────────────────┐
                    │  1. Preparation │
                    └─────────────────┘
      ┌──────────────┐          ┌──────────────┐
      │ 4. Fine-Tuning│         │ 2. Performance│
      └──────────────┘          └──────────────┘
                    ┌─────────────────┐
                    │  3. Assessment  │
                    └─────────────────┘
```

We'll use the pillar "The Cycle of Excellence" to guide us through this lesson.

1. Preparation

So what is this preparation stage all about? Preparation is about doing everything you can to make the most of the pending learning opportunity. Its purpose is to give you a checklist of activities that direct you through the preparation process. This is important, because if you show up unprepared for a learning opportunity, chances are you will not experience the full effect of the learning. The benefit for you is to give you an edge on your hungry competition. The average student does little or nothing to prepare for a learning opportunity. Don't be average. Instead, be exceptional! You can apply these preparation-stage competencies in advance of *every* learning opportunity you encounter from this point on.

Learning starts long before a learning event. Therefore, well in advance of a learning event, it is important to ask yourself, "What is the *desired outcome*? What is my *motivation*? *Why* do I want or need to learn this?" Decide on the learning platform. Is this a class you want to take? Is this class worth it? Does this class cover what you need? Decide whether the class is worth your investment of money, time, and effort. Make sure you are putting your energy into the best situation possible. Choose the best learning platform and program for you at this time.

Before every learning opportunity, there is much you can and need to do to make the learning event as productive and enjoyable as possible. In preparation for each learning event, be sure to do the following:

- Think the subject through.
  - What do I *expect* from this program?
  - What do I *need* from this program?
  - What can I study, read, and watch to prepare for this program?
  - What can give me a learning advantage going into the program?
- Mentally prepare for the program. Put yourself in the *absorbing* mode.
- Prepare to put aside all potential distractions.
- Thoroughly understand the logistics—what, when (date and time), where, and who will be leading the session.
- Thoroughly complete any preprogram assignment(s).
- Complete any participant preprogram survey (if one is provided).
- Promptly respond to preprogram questionnaires and communications from your learning providers.
- Follow all preprogram instructions.

- Understand what materials and implements/devices you need to bring to the program. If that involves an electronic device, be sure to bring along its power supply.
- If the learning opportunity involves an live instructor (versus self-paced online learning), communicate with the instructor.
  - Let him or her know what is at stake for you.
  - Communicate that you are counting on him or her.
  - Communicate what you *need.*
  - Communicate any *special needs* you may have.
  - Communicate about how the subject matter specifically applies to your job.
  - Communicate how important the subject matter is to your ability to perform.
  - Ask questions.
  - Respond to the instructor's questions.

If you don't receive communication from your instructors, you need to reach out and *communicate with them*! The average participant doesn't interact with the instructor before a learning event. Don't be average. Stand out. Be outstanding!

Your performance is going to continuously affect your livelihood and your life. So don't leave it to the mercy of others. Don't settle for less than the very best. If you do settle for less than the best, it can impact you (sometimes in a small way, sometimes in a big way) for the rest of your working life. Challenge your learning providers to give you what you need to perform your work.

Use these checklists to ensure you don't forget anything.

Well in Advance of the Learning Session Checklist

Complete your preparation

___ Verify receipt of participant presession survey (if applicable)

___ Complete participant presession survey (if one is provided)

___ Prepare questions for trainer

___ Communicate with trainer verbally or via e-mail

___ Complete presession assignment(s)

___ Promptly respond to presession questionnaires and communications from your learning provider

___ Follow all presession instructions

Thoroughly understand any logistics

___ Security access to building and/or training room

___ Parking

___ Start time

___ Training location address

___ Training room number

___ End time

___ Location contact information

Know what you need to bring to the session

___ Laptop or tablet (don't forget the power supply)

___ Props

___ Materials

___ Visuals

___ Other

Figure 5.1

Well in Advance of *Virtual* Learning Session Checklist

___ If the virtual session is to be instructor-led, follow the *complete your preparation* steps as noted above.

Virtual Connections

___ Receive the connection information to the virtual platform (Typically a web address, URL)

___ Do a complete pre-check of the connection

___ Make sure to have a strong, reliable connection

___ Assure your device is equipped to connect to the virtual platform. Make adjustments as necessary

___ Prepare microphone and camera (if applicable)

___ Understand how to navigate the platform

Thoroughly understand the virtual logistics

___ Start and end time of the event

___ Log-in information (typically username and password)

___ Understand the protocol for asking questions (if applicable)

Figure 5.2

SURVEY

When it comes to training preparation,

    a) I am always comprehensively prepared.

    b) I never give it much thought.

    c) I'm too busy to prepare.

    d) I figure I can catch up during the session.

What to Expect and What to *Demand*—1

Be prepared to receive a session introduction from the learning provider. Be prepared to listen for and understand the following information.

The Session Introduction

1. What is [insert the course title here]?
2. What is its purpose?
3. Why are we implementing this?
   - Problem
   - Opportunity
   - Weakness
   - Compliance
4. What are the implications of not acting now?
5. Why are we using this particular approach?
6. What is the evidence supporting it? (Prove it!)
7. What's in it for you? (WIIFY)
8. What are some examples of its practical application?
9. What is the expected outcome?
   "By the end of this session, you will know how to _____."

Figure 5.3

The Session Introduction is an overall introduction to the learning session. We will delve into these steps in detail when we get to the performance stage of *The Cycle of Excellence.*

If you don't receive a session introduction, prepare to *ask* for one! Hold your learning provider accountable. Your livelihood is at stake!

What to Expect and What to *Demand*—2

For each lesson that will be covered in the session, be prepared to receive a lesson format, which includes the items listed in the following figure.

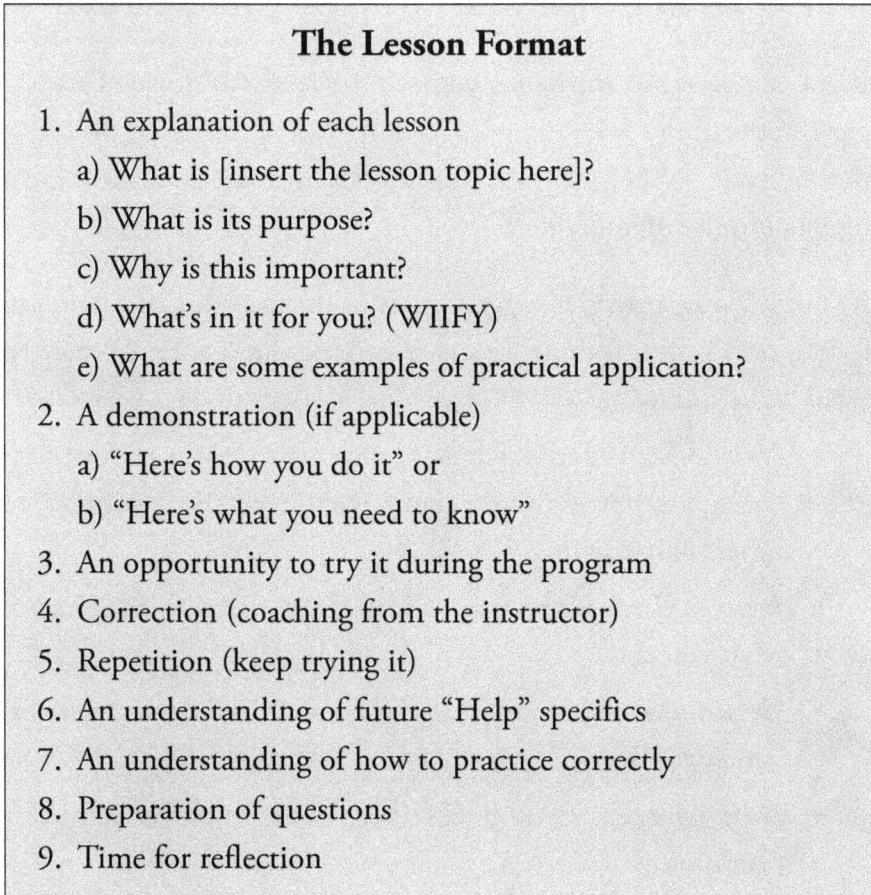

The Lesson Format

1. An explanation of each lesson
   a) What is [insert the lesson topic here]?
   b) What is its purpose?
   c) Why is this important?
   d) What's in it for you? (WIIFY)
   e) What are some examples of practical application?
2. A demonstration (if applicable)
   a) "Here's how you do it" or
   b) "Here's what you need to know"
3. An opportunity to try it during the program
4. Correction (coaching from the instructor)
5. Repetition (keep trying it)
6. An understanding of future "Help" specifics
7. An understanding of how to practice correctly
8. Preparation of questions
9. Time for reflection

Figure 5.4

The lesson format is a solid guideline for helping you understand the lesson. Once again, we will explore these steps in detail when we get to the performance stage of *The Cycle of Excellence*.

If you don't receive these key points and these opportunities, prepare to ask for them. Be proactive. Go after your future with passion!

There will be more on *The Lesson Format* later in the chapter.

Prepare to Deliver Your Compelling Introduction

If you are asked to introduce yourself, be ready to do so. This is a great opportunity for some recognition. You never know who is in the room or online. Consider this an opportunity to make a great impression. Be memorable.

If your learning provider suggests an introduction format for you to follow, do so. But nothing says you can't expound a bit. Prepare to include the following key information:

- *Name.* Clearly and slowly state your name. If you are fortunate enough to have a unique name, spell it for the benefit of the others participating.

- *Position.* If you have a title, state it. If not, describe in a sentence what you do.

- *Department.* Communicate the name of the department for which you work.

- *Duration of employment.* "I've been with [employer name] for [duration]."

- *Key responsibilities.* "My key responsibilities include _____." Succinctly describe up to three of your most important responsibilities.

- *Your value.* "The value I offer [employer name] is _____." This is where you have an opportunity to shine. Be ready to communicate your value. Carefully think this through. (Reference "The Value You Offer" in chapter 3, "You Enterprises.")

- *Hobbies/Fun Fact.* "When I'm not working, I enjoy _____." Offer a little bit about you, the person (not the performer).

Your compelling introduction can be the first step to a promotion or an opportunity. Deliver your compelling introduction with confidence and poise. Once again, you never know who might be listening. Prepare to deliver your compelling introduction concisely. Take one minute at the most.

SURVEY

If someone asked you, "What *value* do you bring to your organization?"...

a) I'd be ready with an accurate, well-thought-out answer.

b) I'd make my answer up on the fly.

c) I'd have no idea how to answer.

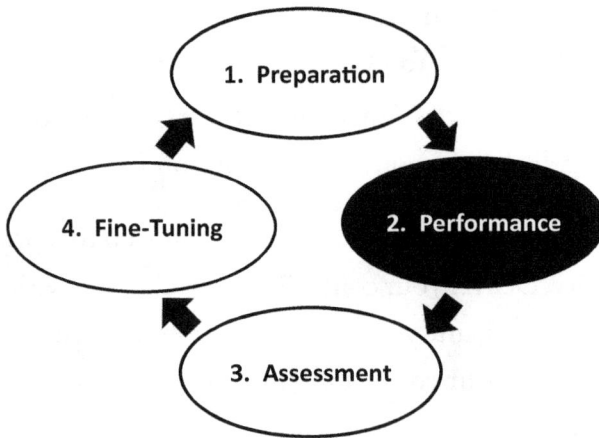

2. Performance

It's time to learn. It's time for the learning event. A learning event should be delivered in a fashion similar to this:

1. a focused launch

2. your compelling introduction

3. the session introduction

4. the lesson format, which includes, for each lesson, the lesson explanation and a lesson demonstration

So What Is This Performance Stage All About?

Maximum Positive Impact Performance means *actively* participating in a training event. The steps presented in this stage will ensure that you are actively involved in the learning opportunity. The purpose of this stage is to maximize your learning and to ensure a richer learning experience, to guarantee that you receive the knowledge and skills you need, and to make sure that the skills and knowledge you gain are transferable to your on-the-job performance.

Performance during the learning event is paramount, because if you are not actively involved, you won't receive the maximum benefit of the event. If you do not receive knowledge and skills, or if you internalize them in a way that is not transferable to your actual job performance, the training opportunity will have failed.

You will benefit from knowing with confidence that you will perform (during the learning opportunity) with maximum positive impact. You will enjoy the peace of mind that comes with realizing that you're giving the learning event your best effort. Your reputation as a performer and the value-added importance you offer as a contributor to your organization's success will shine through. You are strongly encouraged to *perform* (get actively involved) whenever you have an opportunity to learn.

So how *will* you perform during the learning event?
- What can you *do* during the event to maximize learning?
- How will you *actively* participate?
- Will you attempt to answer questions?
- Will you volunteer to participate in skill drills?

How *will* you make the most of the learning opportunity? Here are some imperatives.

Be Punctual

One of the first and simplest steps you can take is to show up *early*. Be there. Be prompt. It is almost impossible to be precisely *on time*—you're either early or you're late. So be early.

Through the years, I've noticed that the same people tend to be early, and the same people tend to be late. Not being on time can and often does affect others. They need to scramble to cover for you. Besides, being late is inconsiderate and inconvenient to others. It's basically saying, "My time is more valuable than yours." So be early.

I once had a training assignment that was a sixty-mile drive from my home. The weather forecast the night before predicted a major winter storm. With that insight, I left hours early the next morning. I carefully navigated my way through the snowy, icy streets. I got to the site a few hours early. I did my preparation and setup, and then sat back with a cup of coffee and relaxed, waiting for the students to appear. About a half hour prior to the start time, one student showed up. The rest of the students—who, by the way, had traveled from various parts of the world to take part in the event at a significant cost to their employer—showed up either hours late or not at all. Their excuse? The winter storm. Well, if one student got there on time, all of them could have gotten there on time. They were all staying at the same hotel, which incidentally was a ten-minute drive from the training location!

The one gentleman who had showed up early had separated himself from the pack. How did he use his extra time? He spent it asking thoughtful questions about the topic of the upcoming class. We had a very interesting and passionate discussion. This man had planned ahead. He made the best use of his time and got a lot of added value from it.

Be early.

LS—Med—CU

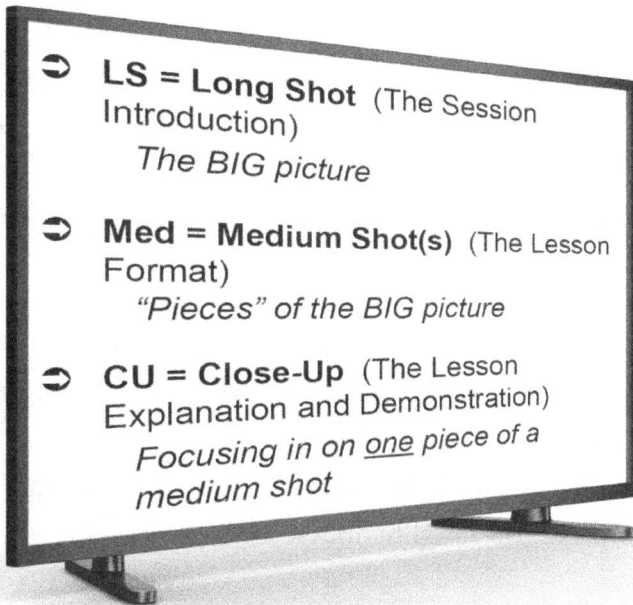

Figure 5.5

Learning Perspective

When receiving new information, it's important to have perspective. You need context. Broadcast media (television) has known this for decades. Broadcast media communicates with us through LS, Med, and CU.

For example, if broadcast media wants to focus on a witness in a courtroom, they don't initially zoom in for a close-up of the witness. We, the audience, wouldn't know who that person is or what that person represents. Instead, the cameraperson starts with a long shot from the back of the courtroom (showing the judge, the attorneys, and the witness) for only one or two seconds. Next, he or she gives us a medium shot of maybe the judge and the witness together in one frame (again, only for a couple of seconds). Then, the cameraperson zooms in for a close-up of the witness. Now, we in the audience have perspective.

As performers, we need to receive new information the same way. Too many learning providers start with close-ups. They then continue with close-up after close-up. Hold them accountable. Make sure they provide you with perspective. If you don't receive a similar perspective, ask for it!

OK, you are about to actively participate in an instructor-led (whether face-to-face or virtual) learning opportunity. Imagine that you are about to *receive* a lot of new information. Your first and super important key role is that of world-class listener. This critical skill will benefit you in the classroom, your place of work, and at home. Listen in order to thoroughly understand, not to respond.

The Communication Process

The following is an example of a typical *voice-to-ear* communication.

1. The communicator (the other person) *sends a message.* The message might be mumbled. The communicator might ramble on and on. He or she might use jargon, acronyms, or buzzwords with which you are not familiar.

2. The receiver (you) *receives a message.* Maybe you are not paying full attention. Maybe you are distracted. Perhaps you are paying full attention, but the message sent by the communicator is jumbled, camouflaged by static, or just not clearly spoken. Perhaps there are language barriers. Background noise also can get in the way. If you're like me, you might have rock-and-roll ears. Rock-and-roll ears come from many years of listening to loud music. The result

is trouble hearing because of never-ending ringing in the ears. (But I wouldn't have given the music up for anything!)

3. The receiver (you) *interprets the message* you think you heard. You interpret the communicator's meaning. Perhaps he or she used terms or words like *ASAP, huge opportunity, important, critical, later*. You interpret them to mean what you think they mean.

4. The receiver (you) *evaluates the message* you think you heard. You might evaluate the message to be good/bad, right/wrong, critical/ not critical, valuable/not valuable, or important/not important.

5. The receiver (you) *responds*. Your response might or might not be immediate. You might require time and effort to form a response. You might need to give it some thought. The response might be relevant, on target, and accurate—or it might be just the opposite.

All five of these steps can cause misunderstanding and miscommunication, leading to a breakdown in communication. When communication failures occur, they happen somewhere in this process. You need to be sure there is no miscommunication by *verifying* what you think you heard.

What Is Involved in the Verification Process?

First and foremost, *focused listening* is involved. Listen as if the communicator is the only person in the universe. Give him or her the gift of your total and complete focus by listening in order to thoroughly understand.

Next, to ensure there is no miscommunication, *paraphrase* back to the speaker what you think you just heard. Use lead-in phrases such as, "Let me make sure I've got this…" Then, paraphrase what you just heard the communicator say. This proves to the *communicator* that "you got it." This proves to *you* that "you got it."

Nothing bad can happen when you paraphrase back to someone to verify understanding. Three things can happen:

1. The communicator will say, "*Yes*, you got it."

2. The communicator will add additional information by saying something like, "*Yes*, and another thing…"

3. The communicator will say, "*No*, that's not what I meant. Let me explain again."

All are positive responses, even the "no." Getting a "No, that's not what I meant" is one of the best things that can happen when you are verifying something. Right then and there, any miscommunication is cleared up. A lot of time and effort can be saved as a result.

Here's a tip: take notes to help you capture what you're hearing. Unless you have an exceptional memory, it's almost impossible to recall everything the speaker is saying. Notes assist you in verifying what you heard.

I once had an opportunity to deliver sales training to a major home-improvement corporation. This sales training was broken down over a three-year period. In year one, I covered the focused-listening and validation process. In year two, to deliver stage two of the training, I traveled back to the same town just outside of Pittsburgh, Pennsylvania. To kick off stage two, I did a quick review of what I had covered in stage one. When I started to review the focused-listening and validation process, a manager in the back of the room stood up and said, "I'd like to say something about this." He went on to say that the people who had become really good at this had reduced their sales cycle by 70 percent! He went on to clarify that "where those individuals used to average ten different contacts to close a sale, they have now reduced it down to an average of three." The salespeople thoroughly understood their prospects' needs, concerns, and objections. They knew how to get their prospects to voice all of their concerns and could confirm their understanding. Then, the salespeople did what they had to do to resolve the issues, and presented their revised solutions to their prospective customers. By listening and verifying, they didn't have to go back and forth nearly as much, which greatly reduced the time and effort they required to close a sale.

SURVEY

On a scale of one to ten, with ten being a great listener and one being a poor listener, I consider myself a _____ .

The Focused Launch

Receive and clearly understand a focused launch of the overall program. Much of this focused launch is what you prepared to receive in the preparation stage.

The Focused Launch

1. The Trainer Introduction
2. The Session Introduction
   a) What is [insert the course title here]?
   b) What is its purpose?
   c) Why are we implementing this?
      - Problem
      - Opportunity
      - Weakness
      - Compliance
   d) Implications of not acting now
   e) Why this particular approach?
   f) Evidence (prove it)
   g) What's in it for you? (WIIFY)
   h) Examples of practical application
   i) The outcome
   "By the end of this session, you will know (how to) _____."
3. The agenda
4. The time line
5. Logistics/site information
6. Ground rules
7. What you'll learn (key, specific takeaways)

> 8. How you'll learn
> 9. Questions
> 10. Your compelling introduction

Figure 5.6

It is important at the start of a learning event to understand the direction the event will take. Listen for and clearly understand *The Focused Launch* of the event. You need to know the following:

1. *The trainer introduction.* Who is he or she, and what are his or her qualifications?

2. *The session introduction.* I will discuss this further in a moment.

3. *The agenda.* Where is this event going?

4. *The time line.* Understand the timing parameters and strictly adhere to them.

5. *Logistics/site information.* Where are the emergency exits, restrooms, break areas, and refreshment areas? What are the parking rules and regulations, and safety rules and regulations?

6. *Ground rules.* Are there any? If so, what are they?

7. *What you'll learn.* Verify your understanding of what you will learn. Based on what you accomplished during the preparation stage, you should have a good understanding of this going in. Verify that nothing has changed.

8. *How you'll learn.* Is this a lecture? What tools will be used to solidify learning?

9. *Questions.* What are the ground rules for asking questions? Where/how can you get your questions answered?

10. *Your compelling introduction.* Deliver the introduction you have prepared.

If you do not understand the particulars of these ten points, this may have an impact on the effectiveness of the learning opportunity, your state of mind, and your comfort.

If you don't receive this information, *ask* for it! If you don't understand it, ask for clarification.

Deliver Your Prepared Introduction

Now it's time to *deliver* your compelling, memorable introduction. Give it clearly and with confidence and pride.

This is the introduction you prepared in the preparation stage. As a reminder, here are the components of the introduction.

Your Compelling Introduction

- *Name*
- *Position*
- *Department*
- *Duration of employment*
- *Key responsibilities*
- *Your value*
- *Hobbies/Fun Fact*

Listen for, Receive, and Understand the Session Introduction

In the discussion of *The Focused Launch* above, you probably recognized the session introduction from the preparation stage. This is *The Session Introduction* you have prepared to receive. Now it's time to put it into action. It's time to thoroughly understand the "whats" and "whys" of the session. As a reminder, here is figure 5.3, "The Session Introduction" again.

Revisiting Figure 5.3

The Session Introduction

1. *What is [insert the course title here]?*
2. *What is its purpose?*
3. *Why are we implementing this?*
   - *Problem*
   - *Opportunity*
   - *Weakness*
   - *Compliance*
4. *What are the implications of not acting now?*
5. *Why are we using this particular approach?*
6. *What is the evidence supporting it? (Prove it!)*
7. *What's in it for you? (WIIFY)*
8. *What are some examples of its practical application?*
9. *What is the expected outcome?*
   - *"By the end of this session, you will know how to _____."*

You *need* this information to gain perspective.

Remember the television analogy? The Session Introduction represents the long shot (LS) and gives you the overall perspective on the entire learning session.

Notice that I opened this book in the introduction and presented this session to you using this format.

If you don't receive something similar to a session introduction, ask for answers and information on these key points. If you don't understand, ask for clarification!

Let's take a closer look at the session introduction.

The Session Introduction

1. **What is [insert the course title here]?**

   You must get a short, clear definition of what the session is about. I can't tell you how often this does *not* happen. I would even go so far as to say that it hardly ever happens. Most training starts with the learning provider stating, "Let's get right into our first lesson." No perspective is offered. Make sure you understand what the session is all about. It should start off with something such as, "So what is [insert the course title here]?"

2. **What is its purpose?**

   Why does the class exist? Why is it necessary?

3. **Why are we implementing this (particular training)?**
   - problem
   - opportunity
   - weakness
   - compliance

   If your organization is implementing a new practice with which you must become proficient, it's important to know the *why* behind the *what* to gain perspective.

4. **What are the implications of not acting now?**

   What happens if this learning isn't implemented? *Why* is this critical? *Why* is this urgent?

5. **Why are we using *this* particular approach?**

   Why are we using this particular approach, solution, direction, or methodology as opposed to something else?

6. **What is the evidence supporting it? (Prove it!)**

   What proof is available to validate the answer to the preceding question ("Why are we using this particular approach?")

7. **What's in it for you? (WIIFY)**

   What *is* the benefit to you of learning this new skill or acquiring this new knowledge?

8. **What are some examples of its practical application?**

   How/where you will apply this new knowledge or skill?

9. **What is the expected outcome?**

   "By the end of this session, you will know how to _____."
   Know *what*? Know how to do what?

For Each Lesson, Receive The Lesson Format

Remember *The Lesson Format* (see figure 5.4 below) from the preparation stage? This is the format you have prepared to receive. Now it's time to make sure you get what you planned for.

Revisiting Figure 5.4

The Lesson Format

    1. An explanation of each lesson

       a) What is [insert the lesson topic here]?

       b) What is its purpose?

       c) Why is this important?

d) What's in it for you? (WIIFY)

e) What are examples of practical application?

2. *A demonstration (if applicable)*

  a) "Here's how you do it" or

  b) "Here's what you need to know"

3. *An opportunity to try it during the program*

4. *Correction (coaching from the instructor)*

5. *Repetition (keep trying it)*

6. *An understanding of future "Help" specifics*

7. *An understanding of how to practice correctly*

8. *Preparation of questions*

9. *Time for reflection*

You need to experience (and understand) each of these nine points. This is the *medium shot* (Med) in our television analogy. This is the learning process. This is *learning*, and this is how you "get it." Receive these for *each* lesson in the session.

Let's dig deeper.

The Lesson Format

1. **An explanation of each lesson**

Here, the learning provider must communicate to you a fairly in-depth explanation of what you're about to learn. In face-to-face or live virtual sessions, a discussion often ensues here.

2. **A demonstration (if applicable)**

Here, the learning provider must show you *how* to do it (*if* the lesson involves a skill or *doing* something). This is where you get a look at the skill you are about to learn. It may be a hands-on demonstration if it involves something you can touch. Seeing is believing. Perhaps a video is shown here. I will say more on this later as well.

3. **An opportunity to try it during the program**

The best way to learn a new skill is to do it. Albert Einstein said, "The only source of knowledge is experience." Ask for an opportunity to *try it*.

4. **Correction (coaching from the instructor)**

Solicit feedback. Implore the instructor to be 100 percent honest with you.

5. **Repetition (keep trying it)**

Yes, keep trying it if you can and if time permits. "Repetition is the mother of skill," says Tony Robbins. Here is a great opportunity to teach what you just learned to someone else in the session, if possible. Teaching is a great way to truly grasp something new.

6. **An understanding of future "Help" specifics**

This learning opportunity won't last forever. Once it ends, where can you get help? What are available help sources? Where can you get your questions answered? Make sure you have access to these sources.

7. **An understanding of how to practice correctly**

Perfect practice makes perfect. Ask the instructor for ideas on how to practice correctly. If possible, video yourself practicing the new skill. Record yourself reciting the new knowledge. I often use my phone to video myself when rehearsing a new program or an upcoming presentation. I watch and listen to it over and over to grasp new material and to monitor my delivery. What's more, because I use my phone, the recordings are always with me.

8. **Preparation of questions. Ask the questions you prepared**
Don't hold back. *Get* what you need.

9. **Time for reflection**
So often, there is little time between one lesson and the next. Ask for time to reflect on what you just learned. Review your notes. Internalize the lesson. Picture yourself applying the new knowledge or skill.

Listen for and Understand "The Lesson Explanation"
The Lesson Explanation

Step one of the lesson format is to receive an *explanation* of the lesson. The Lesson Explanation represents part one of the close-up (CU) in our television analogy. The explanation should cover the following five key points.

The Lesson Explanation

- What is [insert the lesson topic here]?
- What is its purpose?
- Why is this important?
- What's in it for you? (WIIFY)
- What are some examples of its practical application?

Figure 5.7

Expect and understand an *explanation* for each lesson in the session. You need this information to maximize learning.

1. **What is [insert the lesson topic here]?**

   Get a crystal-clear definition or description of the lesson.

2. **What is its purpose?**

   Why does the lesson exist? Why is it necessary?

3. **Why is this important?**

   Understand why this new skill or bit of knowledge is important in the overall learning session.

4. **What's in it for you?**

   What *are* the benefits of this new skill or bit of knowledge for you?

5. **What are some examples of its practical application?**

   How/where you will apply this new knowledge or skill?

If you don't receive an explanation of a lesson, ask for it! If you don't understand it, ask for clarification.

Watch and Understand "The Demonstration"

Expect and understand a *demonstration* for each lesson in the session. You need this information to ensure you comprehend fully.

The Lesson Demonstration

Step two of the lesson format is to receive a *demonstration* of the lesson. The Lesson Demonstration represents part two of the close-up in our television analogy.

The Lesson Demonstration

- "Here's how you do it" or
- "Here's what you need to know"

Figure 5.8

Watch the demonstration, learn, and ask questions. In some cases, you might need to *listen* to the demonstration, learn, and ask questions.

If you don't receive a demonstration, *ask* for one! If you don't understand it, ask for clarification.

Actively Participate

The average participant sits in silence. Don't be that average participant. Instead, actively take part.

- Respond to questions.
- Ask questions.
- Do the hands-on exercises.
- Volunteer to teach the person next to you.
- Ask for help.

Learning leaders will feed off your energy and enthusiasm, which will make for a richer experience for all involved.

Do not accept *not* learning. Your livelihood and reputation are at stake.

As the learning session is coming to a close, confirm the outcome.

- Did I receive what I needed and expected?
- Do I understand?
- Can I convert what I learned to on-the-job performance?

If you answer no to any of these questions, tell the learning provider that you need further assistance. *Don't relent until you get it!*

Understand "How to Follow Through"

- Specifically, where can I get/find help?
- Get specifics regarding coaching and support (understand what to expect).
- Understand how to practice correctly.

Understand "The Closing"

- Receive and thoroughly understand *specific next steps*. If you don't receive specific next steps, *ask* for them! If you don't understand, ask for clarification.
- Complete the assessment honestly.
- Get the learning provider's contact information.

A Note about Virtual Learning

Before we move forward, here are a few thoughts about virtual learning. Much of the learning you receive from this point forward in your career is going to be virtual. I often train instructors on how to instruct people virtually. Every instructor's number one concern by far is "How do we keep them engaged? How do we know what they're doing out there? The students might be texting, tweeting, reading e-mail, playing with the dog...who knows?" Yes, there are a lot of potential distractions out there. I implore you as a virtual student to resist those temptations. Be *present*. You might learn something that can change your life for the better. You don't want to be focused elsewhere when that something is revealed.

Paradigm Shift

Up until now, keeping participants engaged throughout a virtual learning session (or any learning opportunity) was thought to be squarely the instructor's responsibility. However, I'm telling you now—it's *not* the instructor's sole responsibility. Rather, *it is your responsibility to remain engaged.* Who loses if you're not involved in your learning? Don't wait for the instructor to capture your attention. What if he or she does *not* grab your attention? You *need* to learn. Be engaged. Your livelihood depends on it.

Close the door. Put a "Do Not Disturb—Virtual Learning in Progress" sign on your door. Do this even when you are at home. Do this particularly when you are at home! Save e-mail and texting for later. Avoid interruptions. Be present. Much is at stake.

OK, you *prepared* prior to and *performed* during the training session. How did you do?

SURVEY

When it comes to actively participating in a training session,
- a) I always actively participate.
- b) I participate if I'm forced to.
- c) I tend to sit in the back of the room and not get involved.

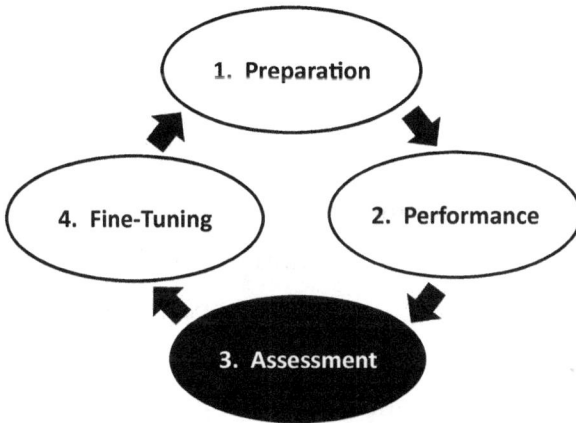

3. Assessment

Now we are going into rarified air: stage three. Assessment actually involves *self-assessment* of your preparation and performance for the learning event you just completed. Average learners do not do this. Once again, don't be average. Step away from the average and do the things that powerful performers do. Do the little things that will affect in a big way your productivity and the value you offer.

At this stage, you should ask, "How did I do with my *preparation* and *performance* for this learning opportunity?" And always ask yourself, "What did I learn?"

- What did I learn about my preparation?
- What did I learn about my performance?

What a great question to ask yourself after every experience—"What did I *learn?*"

The Maximum Positive Impact Assessment stage means assessing your *preparation* prior to the training session and your *performance* during the training session. The purpose of this stage is to help you become aware of possible gaps in your preparation or performance that might have inhibited your learning. This is important, because you need to close those gaps for future learning opportunities. In this way you benefit by assuring yourself that you *never settle for just "good enough."* This is an important step in making sure you are doing everything possible to make the most of your learning opportunities so that you can perform well on the job. Be highly aware of your efforts in the preparation and performance stages. An example of a practical application in which you will use the Assessment stage is after completing each and every learning opportunity.

Below are two tools to help you perform a self-assessment of your preparation and performance after completing each learning opportunity.

Learner Self-Assessment		
Session Name:		
Session Date:		
On a scale of 1 to 10, enter a score in the appropriate box 10 = High, True, Often 1 = Low, False, Not Often		
1	I completed my presession assignments	0
2	I completed the participant presession survey (if applicable)	0
3	I communicated with the learning provider prior to the session	0
4	I understood and had no problem with the logistics	0
5	Overall, I was thoroughly prepared for the learning session	0
6	I delivered a clear, concise and compelling self-introduction	0
7	I actively participated in the learning session	0
8	If I didn't understand, I asked verification questions	0
9	I openly accepted coaching during the try-it exercises	0
10	I understand where I can get help on the session topic(s)	0

11	I understand the type of coaching I can expect from this point forward	0
12	I clearly understand specific next steps	0
13	I understand how to practice correctly	0
14	Overall, I am satisfied with *my* preparation and performance in this learning opportunity	0
	Overall Learner Self-Assessment AVERAGE	0.0

What did I *learn* about my Preparation and Performance for this learning opportunity?

What did I do well?

For future learning opportunities, I'd like to improve in the area(s) of

What can I do differently to make learning opportunities more relevant for me?

Figure 5.9

Next, keep an *ongoing* record.

Learner Self-Assessment Summary **Average of Ten Learning Opportunities Completed**											
On a scale of 1 to 10, enter a score in the appropriate box **10 = High, True, Often 1 = Low, False, Not Often**											
		Learning Opportunities									
Learning Opportunity Number		1	2	3	4	5	6	7	8	9	10	Avg
1	I completed my presession assignments	0	0	0	0	0	0	0	0	0	0	0
2	I completed the participant presession survey (if applicable)	0	0	0	0	0	0	0	0	0	0	0
3	I communicated with the learning provider prior to the session	0	0	0	0	0	0	0	0	0	0	0

4	I understood and had no problem with logistics	0	0	0	0	0	0	0	0	0	0	0
5	Overall, I was thoroughly prepared for the learning session	0	0	0	0	0	0	0	0	0	0	0
6	I delivered a clear, concise and compelling self-introduction	0	0	0	0	0	0	0	0	0	0	0
7	I actively participated in the learning session	0	0	0	0	0	0	0	0	0		0
8	If I didn't understand, I asked verification questions	0	0	0	0	0	0	0	0	0	0	0
9	I openly accepted coaching during the try-it exercises	0	0	0	0	0	0	0	0	0	0	0
10	I understand where I can get help on the session topic(s)	0	0	0	0	0	0	0	0	0	0	0
11	I understand the type of coaching I can expect from this point forward	0	0	0	0	0	0	0	0	0	0	0
12	I clearly understand specific next steps	0	0	0	0	0	0	0	0	0	0	0
13	I understand how to practice correctly	0	0	0	0	0	0	0	0	0	0	0
14	Overall, I am satisfied with *my* preparation and performance in this learning opportunity	0	0	0	0	0	0	0	0	0	0	0
	Learning Opportunities AVERAGE	0	0	0	0	0	0	0	0	0	0	0.00

What did I *learn* about my preparation and performance throughout these ten learning opportunities?

What did I do well?

For future learning opportunities, I'd like to improve in the area(s) of

What can I do differently to make learning opportunities more relevant for me?

Figure 5.10

This Learning Opportunities Summary Tool will help you assess yourself over time. How are you doing? By honestly completing these self-assessments regarding your learning opportunities, you will be taking a big step toward maximizing your ability to learn and delivering on-the-job performance excellence.

SURVEY

When it comes to assessing my preparation and performance of a learning opportunity,

   a) I always do it.
   b) I sometimes do it.
   c) I never do it.
   d) I will do it from this point forward.

So what do you do with this assessment information?

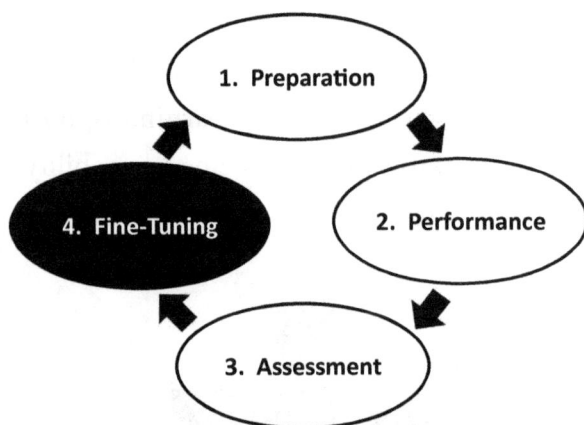

4. Fine-Tuning

What is Maximum Positive Impact Fine-Tuning all about? It's about the action you take to improve your preparation and performance for the very next learning opportunity. The purpose of this stage is, once again, never settling for "good enough." It's important to you, because this is how you continuously grow. The fine-tuning stage ensures that you have an even better and more valuable learning experience the next time. Complete the Learner Fine-Tuning Action Plan after completing each self-assessment.

Take the results from your self-assessment tools and strategize the adjustments you will make for your next opportunity to prepare and perform before and during your next learning opportunity. It's what you *do* with your assessment results that matters.

Let's look at the Learner Fine-Tuning Action Plan tool.

Learner Fine-Tuning Action Plan
Based on: Figure 5.9: Learner Self-Assessment   Figure 5.10: Learner Self-Assessment Summary: Average of   Ten Learning Opportunities Completed
To Fine-Tune My Learning Opportunities PREPARATION, I will:
Specific action:
Action completion date:
Practice opportunity:
Coach who will observe and provide feedback:
To Fine-Tune My Learning Opportunities PERFORMANCE, I will:
Specific action:
Action completion date:
Practice opportunity:
Coach who will observe and provide feedback:

Figure 5.11

SURVEY

When it comes to fine-tuning my preparation and performance after assessing a learning opportunity,

    a) I always do it.

    b) I sometimes do it.

    c) I never do it.

    d) I will do it from this point forward.

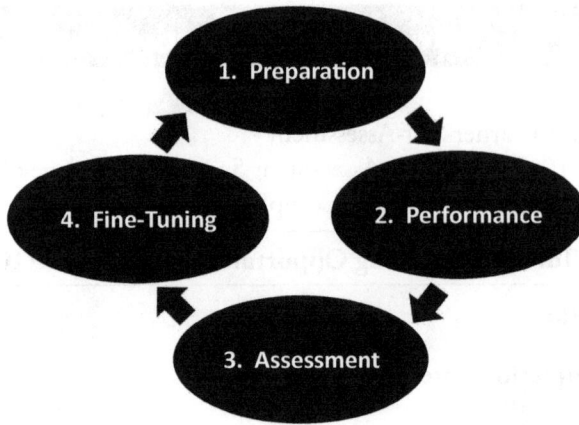

Diagram showing a cycle: 1. Preparation → 2. Performance → 3. Assessment → 4. Fine-Tuning → back to 1. Preparation

In Closing

By implementing the steps in the preparation, performance, assessment, and fine-tuning stages of the "How to Learn with Maximum Positive Impact" competency, you will assure yourself that you have done everything possible to

a) truly acquire essential knowledge and skills; and

b) best position yourself to convert knowledge and skills into high-quality, on-the-job performance.

CHAPTER SUMMARY

- All *learning opportunities* are *not equal* in their effectiveness.

- All *learning providers* are *not equal* in their effectiveness.

- There is too much inconsistency and ineffectiveness in the quality of training.

- Inconsistency and ineffectiveness are unacceptable. Be *actively involved* in your own development.

- Prepare, perform, assess, and fine-tune your learning involvement to maximize your learning and retention. Your livelihood and well-being depend on it.

CALL TO ACTION

1. Go to Appendix A of this book and order your free copy of the **Well-Being at Work Toolkit**. The toolkit includes the following:
   - The Learner Self-Assessment tool (Figure 5.9)
   - The Learner Self-Assessment Summary: Average of Ten Learning Opportunities Completed tool (Figure 5.10)
   - The Learner Fine-Tuning Action Plan tool (Figure 5.11)

2. Print, in color, the **Well-Being at Work Quick Reference Card**. Have it laminated at your local office supply store. Keep it visible to help you stay on track.

3. With the quick reference card in hand, prepare, perform, assess, and fine-tune your next learning opportunity and every learning opportunity from this point forward.

4. Visit www.MPimpact.com to follow and contribute to our blog. Stay progressive.

Go forth and learn with Maximum Positive Impact!

SURVEY

Will I implement the call to action above?
   a) Yes, right now!
   b) No.
   c) Hmm…maybe later.

REFLECTION

To *embed* the knowledge and skills just learned, answer the following questions.

1. *What* did I learn?
   • How can I apply this knowledge to my work?

   • How will it make me more efficient?

- How can this information help me provide better customer service?

- How can this insight make me more valuable?

2. *How, when,* and *where* can I *follow through* to stay progressive and maintain these skills? (Practice in my attempt to perfect them.)

3. *How, when,* and *where* can I *apply* the knowledge I acquired and *perform* the skills I have learned?

Chapter 6

Action 2: How to *Follow Through* with Maximum Positive Impact

You have to apply yourself each day to becoming a little bit better.
By applying yourself to the task of becoming a little better each and
every day over a period of time, you will become a LOT better.
—John Wooden

Follow-Through

This is an essential ingredient in getting and staying gainfully employed. Without it, consistent gainful employment is at risk.

Top performers, people who are of great importance to their employers, stay progressive. They follow through to make the knowledge and skills learned part of their value portfolio.

The Power Unit
(*The Power of Three*)

You, the Performer

Learning Provider   **Coach/Mentor**

The coach/mentor, another key function of the Power Unit, is the focus of this competency. Your function in this action is to follow through (you are the coachee).

- Learning – Follow-through = Unlikely knowledge and skills retention.
- Unlikely knowledge and skills retention leads to unlikely on-the-job performance excellence.
- Unlikely on-the-job performance excellence leads to potential job loss.

What Is Follow-Through?

Follow-through is what must happen after a learning event. Any time you learn something of value, you must decide what you will do with that knowledge or skill. It's what occurs after the learning that launches that new knowledge or skill into a place of value. Follow-through is the continuing path to mastery.

Follow-through is doing everything you can to

- progress;
- apply what you've learned to your work;
- stay current (changes, innovations, improvements, additions);
- master your area(s) of expertise;
- stay valuable;
- stay at the top of your game;
- be better; and
- maintain staying power.

Follow-through has to do with converting the specialized knowledge and skills you have learned into consistent, high-quality on-the-job performance. That is easier said than done. Follow-through takes a lot of concentrated effort. Follow-through ensures that you are and will remain at the top of your game.

Don't go it alone. Get help! Use your Power Unit (Pillar 4). Use the power of three instead of attempting this alone. You are ultimately responsible for your own performance. But you should also use your coach and your mentor. Lean on your learning providers. Stay in touch with all of them. Communicate. Your learning providers gave you the initial knowledge and skills. Now, your coaches and mentor will help you follow through. They will help you apply your specialized knowledge and skills. In other words, they will help assure that you perform.

Learning is just the beginning. It's what happens after you acquire new knowledge or a new skill that will make or break your performance. You can easily get lost between Action 1 (Learn) and Action 3 (Perform). Therefore, Action 2 (Follow-Through) exists to keep you on track and to keep you progressive.

For decades, management has lamented, "Why does so much learning *not* stick? Why do so many learning initiatives result in disappointing performance? Why am I not getting a satisfying return on my learning investments?" I believe the answers to these questions involve

a) ineffective learning (see the previous chapter);

b) little or no follow-through; or

c) a lack of *effective* follow-through.

Learning events are just that—learning events. Even though the event *might* be successful, if the knowledge and skills are not applied, the desired outcome—performance—will not be achieved. The desired outcome is always performance (and thus productivity). What happens *after* the learning event is what *assures* performance.

An All-Too-Common Problem

Ineffective, limited, or no follow-through activities, and ineffective or no coaching are common problems that prevent learning from "sticking" and prevent knowledge and skills from being applied.

Often, follow-through involves coaches or mentors. But follow-through is not just about receiving coaching. Follow-through involves many different avenues. Effective follow-through is your responsibility. Don't blame your coaches or the lack of coaching for less-than-stellar follow-through.

Another problem is that all coaches are *not* equally effective. In business, coaching is often an every-now-and-then activity. Or else, coaching is not provided at all. When an employee does receive coaching, it is often to correct something he or she is doing wrong. Although correction is a key part of coaching, effective coaching is so much more. Such problems related to coaching can have an enormous negative effect on your performance, your career, and your well-being.

If you are fortunate enough to receive coaching, you need to ask yourself the following questions:

- How effective are my coaches?
- How effective is their coaching ability?
- How accessible are they?
- Are they knowledgeable in my area of expertise?
- Do they know what A+ performance looks like?
- Do they have the time to coach me?

I'll ask once again: are you willing to chance it? You *might* get consistent, excellent, and effective coaching, or you might not. Are you willing to put your livelihood in the hands of someone who might or might not be effective or available?

Causes

What are the common causes of ineffective follow-through or a lack of follow-through?

1. *Time.* Do you have time to follow through? Do you have the time and energy to stay at the top of your game? How do you best spend your available time and energy?

2. *Priority.* Is follow-through a priority?

3. *Comfort.* Are you comfortable with your abilities? Do you feel you are right where you need to be regarding your knowledge and capabilities? Are you basically comfortable where you are?

4. *Coach's ability.* Does your coach have sufficient coaching knowledge and ability?

5. *Coach's time.* Does your coach have enough time to coach you? Coaching is often provided by the person you report to and only is one of that person's responsibilities. Often, he or she can feel overwhelmed by being asked to do more and more in the same amount of time. Sound familiar?

How Do You Know?

When it comes to coaching, how do you *know* whether or not you are receiving effective coaching? How do you know whether the coach is effective or ineffective, competent or incompetent? You can't leave this to chance.

As in chapter 5, which was about learning providers, this chapter will give you checkpoints. I'll provide techniques and questions to help you ensure that you are receiving true performance-enhancing coaching. You must be certain you are getting effective coaching to give you the best opportunity to perform. If you have a coach who is not delivering what's listed in this chapter, *coach him or her on how to coach you*! Guide them to give you what you need. Hold your coaches accountable. Your occupational and overall well-being depends on it.

What Are the Implications of Ineffective or Absent Follow-Through or Coaching?

The danger is that you will get left behind. As we all know, change is constant. New information comes at us in a continuous flow. New innovations are constant. Updates and upgrades are happening all the time. New, different, and improved ways of doing things are an everyday reality. You *must* stay on top of the changes. You must keep an eye out for pending change. Know it is coming, and see it coming. Don't let change catch you unprepared. Whenever possible, make the necessary adjustments *well ahead* of the impending change. Staying current is paramount, and follow-through keeps you current and relevant.

Good News

The good news is that there is much you can do to follow through effectively. There is much you can do to keep yourself current and relevant. There is much you can do to stay progressive. There is much you can do to ensure you are receiving excellent coaching.

This chapter covers eight key follow-through actions that will increase the likelihood of stellar performance and help keep you current and progressive. Here are the eight **follow-through actions** that will be covered in this chapter.

1. **Receive coaching.**
2. **Keep *it* in front of you.**
3. **Take knowledge and skill-learning refreshers.**
4. **Read.**
5. **Study.**
6. **Quiz yourself.**
7. **Teach, coach, and mentor others.**
8. **Speak or write on your area of expertise.**

SURVEY

Regarding follow-through,

    a) I am a follow-through master.

    b) I follow through when I feel it's necessary.

    c) I am comfortable where I am.

    d) Follow-through?

Let's learn!

The Lesson Introduction

What is this lesson all about?

1. **What is "How to *Follow Through* with Maximum Positive Impact"?**

   "How to *Follow Through* with Maximum Positive Impact" is a lesson focusing on what you can do *before*, *during*, and *after* a follow-through opportunity to maximize retention. It's about expanding knowledge and skills learned so that you can convert them into consistent on-the-job performance excellence. This lesson provides the *processes*, *techniques*, and *tools* you need when preparing for and participating in follow-through.

2. **What is its purpose?**

   The lesson's purpose is to increase the likelihood of you, the performer, delivering sustainable, optimal on-the-job performance. Its aim is to give you tools to keep you current and prepared for change. Its purpose is also to maximize your ability to receive coaching and mentoring.

3. **Why should I implement this approach?**

   You will stay sharp. Nothing bad can happen by doing what this lesson is asking you to do. You must continue to be responsible for your own development. You must be in charge of your own future. Coach John Wooden said, "It's what you learn *after you know it all* that counts."

4. **What are the implications of not acting now?**

   You will be in danger of getting left behind and having change blindside you.

5. **Why should I use *this* particular approach?**

   No one else will take charge of your ability to perform and keep performing. Therefore, *you* must be responsible. Don't simply accept what you are given. Ensure that the coaching you receive is quality coaching. Demand quality coaching!

6. **What is the evidence that this approach works?**

   As with effective learning, you can be the judge when it comes to proving the effectiveness of this action. I won't bury you under an avalanche of information. I am just providing the essentials that drive the success of the action practice.

7. **What's In It For You? (WIIFY)**

   You could become employed or stay employed. You could be even more valuable to your employer and remain current, relevant, and valuable.

8. **What are some examples of its practical application?**

   The practices covered in this lesson will enable you to consistently follow through with maximum positive impact. The practices will give you crystal-clear direction on how to make the most of every *follow-through* opportunity in which you participate from this point forward.

9. **What is the expected outcome?**

By the end of this lesson, you will know how to maximize your follow-through abilities so that you can perform with excellence.

Regarding what you'll read throughout this chapter, keep in mind that your coaches do *not* have to provide the information in the exact formats and in the exact order I've presented them in, and they probably won't. The labels or names I've given to the blocks of information are enclosed in boxes to help you separate the information into understandable segments.

The formats provided will help you

1. experience follow-through in a way that will maximize the effectiveness of the follow-through activity;
2. maximize the likelihood that you will thoroughly understand the coaching interaction; and
3. know what and how coaching should be delivered and what you should be receiving.

Know that the way a coach "unwraps" a new topic or skill will go a long way toward helping you perform. Experiencing coaching in this way makes it as complete a coaching experience as possible. It increases your likelihood of "getting it."

Be alert, and keep your eyes and ears open for this information. If you're not receiving it from your coach/mentor, *ask for it.*

SURVEY

Choose the statement below that best describes how you feel when you receive coaching.

    a) I am grateful for any opportunity to be coached.

    b) It is a necessary evil. Why don't they just leave me alone?

    c) If my coach knew what he or she was doing, I would find it valuable.

    d) What coaching?

The majority of this chapter will be focused on Follow-Through Action 1.

Follow-Through Action 1: Receive Coaching

As mentioned earlier in this book and earlier in this chapter, don't go it alone. Solicit coaching from others. If coaching is provided, make the most of it. If coaching isn't provided, ask for it. If it is still not provided, seek a coach on your own. You can never outgrow your need for a coach. Even the most accomplished performers in the world, in all professions, still employ a coach. Yes, you might be even more talented than your coach—in which case, all the better.

- Coaches keep you on course.
- They won't let you stray.
- Coaches inspire, enable, and encourage.
- They listen.
- They praise.
- Coaches recognize flaws that you can't see.
- They criticize.

- They correct imperfect practice and performance.
- Coaches don't let you fail.

Great coaches are revered. Great coaches can make all the difference in the world when it comes to your performance.

When a coaching opportunity presents itself to you, you will need to do the following.

1. *Prepare* for the coaching interaction.
2. *Perform* (interact with the coach) during the coaching session to maximize its effectiveness.
3. *Assess* your preparation for and performance during the coaching interaction.
4. *Fine-tune* your preparation and performance for the next coaching interaction.

Let's take a detailed look at each stage of "How to *Receive Coaching* with Maximum Positive Impact."

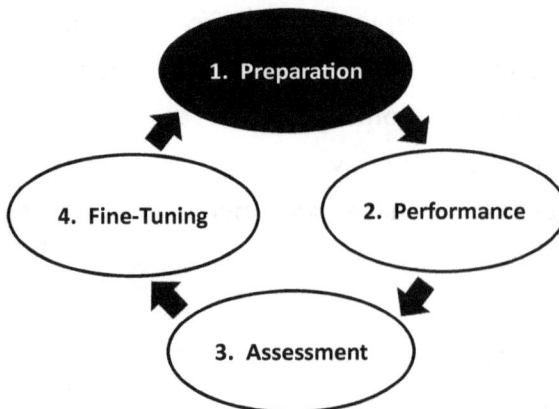

How to *Receive Coaching* with Maximum Positive Impact

1. Preparation

4. Fine-Tuning

2. Performance

3. Assessment

Once again, we'll use the pillar "The Cycle of Excellence" to guide us through this lesson.

1. Preparation

The preparation for a coaching opportunity is similar to the preparation for a learning opportunity. It is about doing everything you can to make the most of a coaching interaction. The purpose of this stage is to give you a checklist of activities that guide you through the preparation process. This is important, because if you show up unprepared for a coaching opportunity, chances are you are not going to experience the full effect of the instruction. The benefit for you is to get the best feedback and direction from the coach you can possibly receive. You can apply these preparation-stage competencies in advance of *every* coaching opportunity you encounter from this point forward.

Know in advance of the coaching session what you want from it. What will make it successful?

Strengths, Weaknesses, and Performance Behaviors

In getting ready for a coaching opportunity, start with the following tasks.

a) Be familiar with your strengths and weaknesses when it comes to performing key job functions. When working at improving a weakness, focus on the liabilities that are toughest and most challenging for you.

b) Know A+ performance acquired from training. Know what A+ performance consists of. What do you need to know about A+ performance? You need to know

- which *behaviors* are associated with A+ performance;
- what A+ performance *looks* like (if applicable);
- what A+ performance *sounds* like (if applicable); and
- what *outcome* needs to have occurred to achieve an A+ performance.

Know A+ performance and its related behaviors inside out. Always work toward perfecting these behaviors. The coach is there to help you.

Know Your Coach

Get to know your coach, and make sure the coach gets to know you. Develop a rapport with him or her. Make sure the coach understands your motivators, both business and personal. Communicate with the coach regarding how and when he or she will *observe* your performance. Understand if, when, and how your coach will *intervene* during your performance.

If you share rapport with the coach, that enables him or her to be candid with you about your performance. You certainly don't want your coach withholding feedback to spare your feelings. Trust is critical. You must trust in your coach. You must know that your performance is his or her number one priority when working with you. Once again, we're talking about your livelihood here.

To be coached with maximum positive impact, make sure your coach understands *you*. Make sure he or she knows where you stand regarding the particular task or job function that will be observed.

Communicate with Your Coach

I will borrow here from the *Goal-Achieving Formula* in chapter 3, "You Enterprises," and say that you should communicate with your coach regarding particular task or job function goals.

Revisiting Figure 3.1

The Maximum Positive Impact Goal-Achieving Formula

1. *Where do I want to be (regarding my goal)? (Figure out exactly what you want. Be very specific.) My specific goal is _____. I will achieve my goal by _____.*

2. *Where am I currently (regarding my goal)?*

3. *What are potential challenges to getting to where I want to be? Why am I not there now?*

4. *Why do I want to be there? What is my motivation? What is the benefit for me?*

5. *Am I primarily looking to relieve existing pain, avoid potential pain, or achieve gain? On a scale of one to ten, how high is my level of urgency to reach my goal? (Without urgency, change is unlikely.)*

6. *What help do I need?*

7. *Do I have the means to get there? If not, how can I acquire the means? What means/resource(s) do I need? Who can help me?*

8. *What have I tried in the past that didn't work? Why didn't it work? What did I learn from those experiences?*

9. *Which aspects of what I tried in the past did work? How can I leverage those successes?*

Do *determination, discipline, focus,* and *measurement* apply when a person is following through? You bet they do—in a huge way!

Help your coach, coach you.

Understand the Maximum
Positive Impact Coaching Process

There are three phases to a coaching interaction. They are

1. your activities *prior* to performing a task;
2. *your performance of a task* while your coach is observing you; and
3. your *receipt of coaching and feedback* based on what your coach observed during your performance.

To help you guide your coach, you should understand the *Maximum Positive Impact Coaching Process.* An optimal coaching opportunity process should look something like what follows.

The Maximum Positive Impact Coaching Process

Phase 1: *Prior* to Performance Observation

  a) Understand what will be observed.

  b) Understand your performance objective.

  c) Understand the coach's intervention strategy.

Phase 2: *During* Performance Observation

  a) Perform the job function.

  b) Expect intervention (if applicable).

Phase 3: *Following* Performance Observation (The Coaching Session)

  a) Understand the coach's *focused launch.*

b) Be prepared for and answer the coach's questions.

c) Listen actively.

d) Receive and understand the coach's point of view.

e) Provide feedback on the coach's point of view.

f) Communicate your recommended plan of action.

g) Listen to and understand the coach's recommended plan of action.

h) Mutually agree on a plan of action or area of development.

i) Discuss the *future*.

j) Verbally summarize the coaching session back to the coach to ensure you have completely understood everything.

Figure 6.1

Let's take a closer look at the *Maximum Positive Impact Coaching Process*.

Phase 1: *Prior* to Performance Observation

a) **Understand what will be observed.** What specific task or job activity will the coach observe? Make sure you both agree on this. How do you feel about your ability to perform the specific task or job activity? On a scale of one to ten, with ten being A+ performance, where would you rank yourself? This is important to understand when you receive coaching. Are you and your coach on the same page?

b) **Understand your performance objective.** What is your performance objective? What is the desired outcome of the task or job activity? Once you completed the task, did you, in your own mind, achieve your desired outcome? Again, it's important that you and your coach see the same thing.

c) **Understand the coach's intervention strategy.** Will the coach step in to help or make comments while you are performing the activity that is the focus of the coaching? If so, plan to discuss this prior to performance. How and when will the coach intervene, if that is the plan? Just so there are no surprises, you both need to agree on the approach.

Phase 2: *During* Performance Observation

a) **Perform the job function.** Carry out the activity as you usually do. This way, the coach will have a baseline of your performance that can be measured against A+ performance, which enables him or her to coach you accordingly.

b) **Expect intervention (if applicable).** This should be based on the agreement in Phase 1(step c) above.

Phase 3: *Following* Performance Observation (The Coaching Session)

In the next stage of the *Maximum Positive Impact Coaching Process*, we delve deeper into phase 3.

It's important as part of your preparation to know the shape the coaching session should take. Know that the coach most likely will not be delivering the coaching session in the exact sequence but that it should in some way include the components of phase 3, as seen in figure 6.1.

Also know that ideally the coach should instruct you differently per task based on your level of expertise for a particular task. If you are skilled at the task, the coaching session should be more collaborative. However, if you are new to a particular task, or if your performance is lacking, the coaching should be more directive.

SURVEY

When it comes to my preparation to receive coaching,
   a) I am always comprehensively prepared.
   b) I never give it much thought.
   c) I'm too busy to prepare.
   d) I don't prepare. I just receive the coaching.

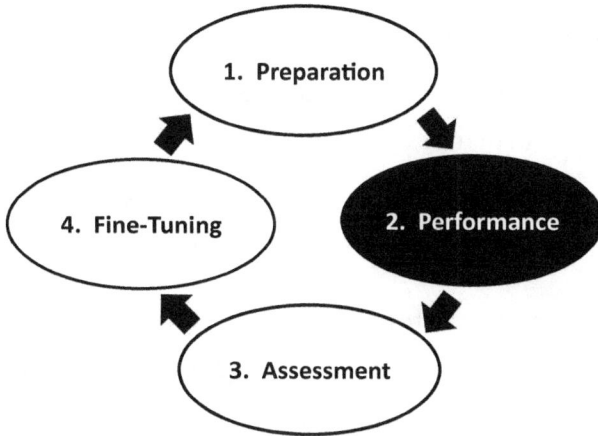

2. Performance

You've carried out the task. The coach has observed you. It is now time for the coaching session, time to receive feedback.

So how do you *perform* during the coaching session? How do you contribute? How do you make the most out of the session?

Perhaps the feedback occurs in real time as you are performing the task. Perhaps the coaching session is separate from the performance. Either way, this performance stage deals with the actual coaching interaction.

So What Is This *Performance* Stage All About?

Maximum Positive Impact Performance means *actively* participating in the coaching interaction. The competencies presented at this stage will ensure that you are actively involved in the coaching opportunity.

During the performance stage, keep the following points in mind.

- Openly *receive* the feedback.
- Don't resist the critique or defend your performance. Quietly receive feedback at this point.
- Be thankful for the feedback, as it is a gift that will enhance your performance.
- Be prepared to respond to the coach's comments when the opportunity presents itself.

The purpose of the performance stage is to maximize your ability to receive coaching to help improve performance. Its objective is also to ensure a richer coaching experience and that the instruction you receive is transferable to on-the-job performance. Performance during the coaching event is important, because if you are not open to feedback and actively involved in the coaching interaction, you won't receive the maximum benefit of the coaching session. If feedback is not received in a way that can be transferred to on-the-job performance, the coaching session will have failed.

By actively participating you'll know that you've made the most of the coaching opportunity.

How *will* you perform during the coaching event?

- What can you do during the coaching session to maximize learning?
- How *will* you actively participate?
- Will you attempt to provide thoughtful answers to your coach's questions?
- How *will* you make the most of the coaching opportunity?

Let's find out.

Phase 3: *Following* Performance Observation (The Coaching Session)

Keep in mind that there are many different coaching methodologies. Consider the following questions regarding your coaches.

- How were they trained to coach?
- What method will they use?
- Have they received training in coaching at all?

Some coaching methodologies are more directive. They are a one-way flow—from *them* to *you*—of information. Some are task-based approaches. Some are based on the coach's strengths, so be flexible. Go with the coach's flow. If the coach's style is more instructional, inquire whether you can ask questions. If yes then ask away!

Let's look at each step of the "*Following* Performance Observation (The Coaching Session)" phase more closely.

a) Understand the coach's focused launch.

Often, a coach will just start providing feedback. In the meantime, you may be trying to catch up, to gain perspective on where he or she is going. The five points listed below are areas that will help you gain perspective on the direction of the session. So if the coach does not provide a focused launch, ask questions to gain perspective. A focused coaching session launch should include

- the coach verbally opening the coaching session;
- the coach explaining and you understanding the *purpose* of the session;
- the coach explaining and you understanding why it's *important*;
- the coach explaining and you understanding *what's in it for you*; and
- the coach explaining and you understanding the *Action Plan.**

  *The Action Plan represents the desired outcome of the coaching session. Understand that at the conclusion of this session, you and your coach must discuss a specific plan of action for you going forward.

b) Be prepared for and answer the coach's questions.

Coaching is a dialogue, not a monologue. Offer your viewpoint by answering the coach's questions. Be honest with your answers. Remember, the effectiveness of a coaching relationship is based on trust. Assess your performance. Communicate your thoughts on

- *your* evaluation of *your* performance;
- what you did well;

- what you could have done better;
- what was the cause of less than A+ performance; and
- what you can do differently next time.

c) Listen actively.

All of the world-class listening skills discussed previously in this book apply here as well.

- Listen! Focus your attention on hearing the coach as though he or she were the only person in the universe. Give him or her (and you) the gift of total and complete focus by listening in order to thoroughly understand.
- Take notes.
- Paraphrase back to the coach what you have heard (to ensure understanding).
- Ask for more.

d) Receive and understand the coach's point of view.

A good coach will

- start with positive behavior feedback;
- offer developmental behavior feedback;
- state the benefits of positive behavior;
- *explain* A+ behavior that is related to performance;
- *demonstrate* A+ behavior related to performance (if possible); and
- ask for your opinion on the feedback he or she has offered.

If you don't receive the coach's input related to these points, ask for them!

e) Provide feedback on the coach's point of view.

At this point, if the coach asks for your perspective on his or her coaching, by all means, provide it. However, if the coach doesn't ask for your thoughts, keep your opinions to yourself. If you have questions here, request permission to ask them.

Do you feel that the coach's feedback is accurate? If not, process it in your own mind and see what you can learn from hearing the coach's point of view. We are often too close to our own performance to see it clearly. Listen to what the coach has to say. Try to see his or her point of view.

f) Communicate your recommended plan of action.

Here, the coach might offer his or her plan of action for you without asking for your input. If you are asked for it, though, give it some careful thought before commenting. Then, state your recommended plan of action, which should be focused on *behavior* fine-tuning. What will you do to fine-tune your performance based on both your assessment and the coach's evaluation of the performance? Ask for his or her assistance or recommendations.

g) Listen to and understand the coach's recommended plan of action.

If the coach offers his or her plan of action for you at this point, great. Absorb it. If not, ask for his or her recommended plan of action. See what the coach recommends.

h) Mutually agree on a plan of action or area of development.

Commit to the mutually agreed-upon plan of action. Write it down. Commit to a date and a time when you will follow through with the plan of action. The specifics of an action plan include answering the following questions.

1. What specific *behaviors* need to be fine-tuned?

2. What specifically will you *do* regarding the specific behaviors?

3. What does that action look or sound like?

4. How will you put the behaviors into practice?

5. How will you know you're making progress?

6. How will you measure and document progress?

7. On what specific date will the action be completed? (This action will be completed by _____.)

8. How/when will the coach observe your progress?

i) Discuss the *future*.

Talk about and commit to when you will both meet again to assess your progress on the plan of action. Get out your calendars and schedule the next meeting.

j) Verbally summarize the coaching session to ensure complete understanding

Wrap up the session by expressing your understanding of the feedback and the next steps. This is your livelihood. Don't *assume* you understand it. Confirm it.

Use a lead-in phrase like, "Let me summarize what we've discussed here to assure my understanding."

Confirm the Outcome

- Did I receive what I needed and expected?
- Do I understand?
- Can I convert what I learned during coaching to on-the-job performance?

If you answered "no" to any of these questions, tell the coach you need further assistance. *Don't relent until you get it!*

Sincerely thank your coaches for their feedback and let them know you're looking forward to the next coaching session. Working with a coach you know and trust offers wonderful dividends. It assures follow-through. It can be invaluable to your ability to remain gainfully employed. It can be a catalyst to you offering tremendous value to the global workforce.

SURVEY

Right now, this is my coaching situation:
- a) I don't have a coach.
- b) I have one, but we rarely meet.
- c) I have a healthy, valuable coaching situation with a great coach.

I don't have a coach, so this is what I'm going to do:
- a) I am going to find one starting *right now.*
- b) I'll continue to go it alone.
- c) I will keep my eyes open for a good coach.

Along with receiving coaching, there are seven more follow-through actions you can take to stay progressive and remain at the top of your game.

Let's now address **Follow-Through Actions** two through eight.

2. Keep *it* in front of you.

3. Take knowledge and skill learning refreshers.

4. Read.

5. Study.

6. Quiz yourself.

7. Teach, coach, and mentor others.

8. Speak or write on your area of expertise.

Follow-Through Action 2:
Keep *It* in Front of You

Remember the teakettle? Keep follow-through front and center. Keep *it* in front of you, with *it* being the current focus of your performance and follow-through. This is your current follow-through goal. Prioritize. Ask yourself, "What must I focus on now?" Then, keep it in front of you. If you put it on the *back burner*, it will *lose steam.*

Follow-Through Action 3:
Take Knowledge and Skill Learning Refreshers

Seek out refresher opportunities. Find ways to reinvigorate your learning. Check with the learning provider. Do they offer refresher classes, either face-to-face or online? Perhaps they offer video-based, self-paced refreshers. If so, indulge. Search for other outside resources.

Follow-Through Action 4: Read

Don't ever stop reading and learning. Find books, newsletters, magazines, trade journals, articles, blogs, and websites that relate to your area of expertise. You can't afford to miss a good book or article. As you read, you'll come up with fresh perspectives. You'll be encouraged. You'll find new, valuable ways of doing things. Drink in the knowledge of the written word.

Confirm your understanding with these follow up questions:
- What was the main point of the article or chapter?
- What were the key takeaways I need to remember?
- What was different about what I read?
- What was controversial?
- What was inspiring?
- What questions do I have?
- Where can I apply this knowledge in my profession?
- *Should* I apply this knowledge in my profession? (Weigh the value.)

Follow-Through Action 5: Study

Study the materials you received at a learning event or prior to an online program in which you participated. Review your notes. Add to your notes based on new information you acquire. Study until it clicks. Study until you can say, "I've got it!"

Follow-Through Action 6: Quiz Yourself

After every follow-through or refresher activity, quiz yourself. Doing so will tell you how much information you've retained. It will tell you where you need to focus more attention. Start by asking yourself your new favorite question:

- What did I learn?

Follow-Through Action 7:
Teach, Coach, and Mentor Others

There is no better way to maximize and maintain your value than to teach, coach, or mentor others. Doing these things not only helps you maintain value but also to retain and enhance the knowledge and skills that are pertinent to your livelihood. Just the act of *preparing* to teach, coach, or mentor others helps you stay sharp.

Stay on the lookout for new information. Be progressive. Keep your eyes on the horizon regarding coming change. Then, prepare your "students" for the coming change. Add value for them. Teaching, coaching, and mentoring others makes you *invaluable*.

Follow-Through Action 8:
Speak or Write on Your Area of Expertise

Be a recognized, go-to subject-matter expert in your field. Be actively involved in contributing to blogs. Start your own blog. Be *the* go-to subject-matter expert in your field. Be a recognized name. Contribute answers to question forums regarding your specialty area. This is a powerful method of networking. You can have hundreds or even thousands of people know your name and respect you as someone highly valuable in your field of knowledge.

Speak at trade shows, conventions, and business meetings. Speak wherever people gather regarding your profession. Speak at associations, clubs, and networking meetings. Once again, these are wonderful opportunities to become a recognized go-to expert in your field.

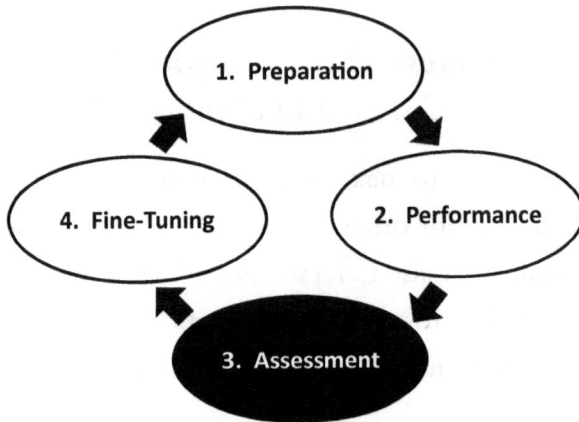

3. Assessment

At the conclusion of a coaching session, ask yourself, "How did I do with my *preparation* and *performance* for this coaching opportunity?" Always ask yourself, "What did I learn?"

- What did I learn about my preparation?
- What did I learn about my performance?

As maximum positive impact performers, we are always asking ourselves, "What did I learn?"

The Maximum Positive Impact Assessment stage means assessing your *preparation* prior to the coaching session and your *performance* during the session. The purpose of this stage is to make you aware of possible gaps in your preparation and performance that might inhibit your follow-through. This is important because you need to close those gaps for future coaching opportunities. The benefit for you is to assure yourself that you *never get left behind*. This is an important step in ensuring that you are doing everything possible to make the most of your follow-through opportunities so that you are always at the forefront of your profession. Be highly aware of your efforts in the preparation and performance stages. Assess your preparation and performance after completing every coaching opportunity.

I've provided two tools to help you self-assess your preparation and performance each time you complete a coaching opportunity.

Coaching Participant Self-Assessment		
Coach Name:		
Session Date:		
On a scale of 1 to 10, enter a score in the appropriate box **10 = High, True, Often 1 = Low, False, Not Often**		
1	Overall, I was thoroughly prepared for the coaching session	0
2	I understood and had no problem with logistics	0
3	I clearly described my performance objective	0
4	I displayed the behaviors associated with A+ performance	0
5	I provided my assessment of my performance openly and honestly	0
6	I participated openly in the coaching conversation	0
7	I reacted well to intervention during my performance of the task (if not applicable, score 10)	0
8	I was open to feedback	0
9	If I didn't understand, I asked verification questions	0
10	I was on target with my recommended action plan	0
11	I thoroughly understood the action plan specifics	0
12	I was attentive and interested during the coaching session	0
13	I verbally summarized the coaching session accurately	0

14	I clearly understood specific next steps	0
15	I will apply the skills and knowledge discussed when performing	0
16	Overall, I am satisfied with my role in this coaching session	0
	Overall Coaching Participant AVERAGE	0.0

What did I *learn* about my Preparation and Performance for this coaching session?

What did I do well?

For future coaching sessions, I'd like to improve in the area(s) of

What can I do differently to make coaching sessions more relevant for me?

Figure 6.2

Next, keep an *ongoing* record.

Coaching Participant Self-Assessment Summary Average of Ten Coaching Sessions Completed												

On a scale of 1 to 10, enter a score in the appropriate box
10 = High, True, Often   1 = Low, False, Not Often

		Coaching Sessions										
	Coaching Session Number	1	2	3	4	5	6	7	8	9	10	Avg
1	Overall, I was thoroughly prepared for the coaching session	0	0	0	0	0	0	0	0	0	0	0
2	I understood and had no problem with logistics	0	0	0	0	0	0	0	0	0	0	0
3	I clearly described my performance objective	0	0	0	0	0	0	0	0	0	0	0
4	I displayed the behaviors associated with A+ performance	0	0	0	0	0	0	0	0	0	0	0
5	I provided my assessment of my performance openly and honestly	0	0	0	0	0	0	0	0	0	0	0

6	I participated openly in the coaching conversation	0	0	0	0	0	0	0	0	0	0	0
7	I reacted well to intervention during my performance of the task (if not applicable, score 10)	0	0	0	0	0	0	0	0	0	0	0
8	I was open to feedback	0	0	0	0	0	0	0	0	0	0	0
9	If I didn't understand, I asked verification questions	0	0	0	0	0	0	0	0	0	0	0
10	I was on target with my recommended action plan	0	0	0	0	0	0	0	0	0	0	0
11	I thoroughly understood the action plan specifics	0	0	0	0	0	0	0	0	0	0	0
12	I was attentive and interested during the coaching session	0	0	0	0	0	0	0	0	0	0	0
13	I verbally summarized the coaching session accurately	0	0	0	0	0	0	0	0	0	0	0
14	I clearly understood specific next steps	0	0	0	0	0	0	0	0	0	0	0
15	I will apply the skills and knowledge discussed when performing	0	0	0	0	0	0	0	0	0	0	0
16	Overall, I am satisfied with my role in this coaching session	0	0	0	0	0	0	0	0	0	0	0
	Coaching Sessions AVERAGE	0	0	0	0	0	0	0	0	0	0	0.00

What did I *learn* about my Preparation and Performance over these ten coaching sessions?

What did I do well?

For future coaching sessions, I'd like to improve in the area(s) of

What can I do differently to make coaching sessions more relevant for me?

Figure 6.3

This Coaching Participant Self-Assessment Summary tool will help you evaluate yourself over time. How are you doing? By honestly completing these self-assessments you will be taking a big step toward maximizing your ability to follow through.

SURVEY

When it comes to assessing my preparation and performance for a coaching session,

   a) I always do it.
   b) I sometimes do it.
   c) I never do it.
   d) I will do it from this point forward.

So what do you do with this assessment information?

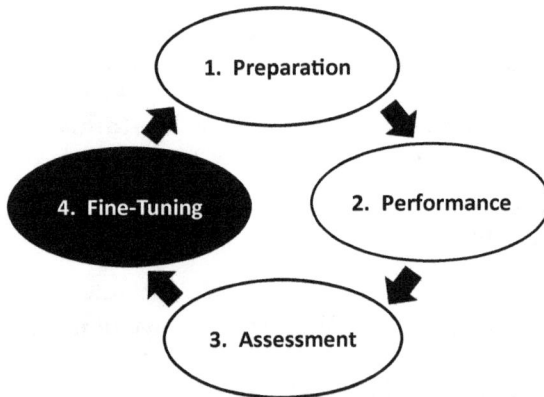

4. Fine-Tuning

How can you improve your preparation and performance for the next coaching opportunity?

158

Use the results from your self-assessment tools to strategize and fine-tune your approach in both areas. Strategize on the adjustments you will make to your preparation and performance before and during your very next coaching session. It's what you *do* with your assessment results that matters.

What is Maximum Positive Impact Fine-Tuning all about? It's about the action you take to improve your preparation and performance for the next coaching opportunity that follows. The purpose of this stage is, once again, never settling for "good enough." It's important to you because this is how you continuously grow. The fine-tuning stage ensures that you have an even better and more valuable coaching experience the next time. This stage helps to ensure better results the next time. Once again, you should complete these self-assessments after every coaching event or opportunity.

Let's look at the Fine-Tuning Action Plan tool.

Coaching Participant Fine-Tuning Action Plan

Based on:
    Figure 6.2: Coaching Participant Self-Assessment
    Figure 6.3: Coaching Participant Self-Assessment Summary: Average
       of Ten Coaching Sessions Completed

To Fine-Tune My Coaching Participant PREPARATION, I will:
Specific action: **Action completion date:** **Practice opportunity:** **Coach who will observe and provide feedback:**

To Fine-Tune My Coaching Participant PERFORMANCE, I will:
Specific action:
Action completion date:
Practice opportunity:
Coach who will observe and provide feedback:

Figure 6.4

SURVEY

When it comes to fine-tuning my preparation and performance after I assess a coaching session,

    a) I always do it.

    b) I sometimes do it.

    c) I never do it.

    d) I will do it from this point forward.

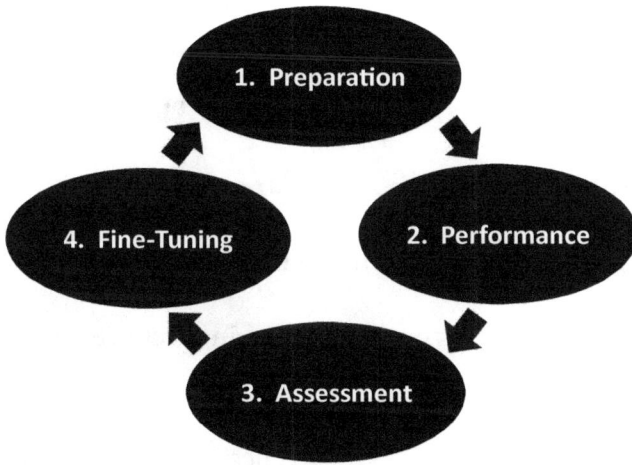

In Closing

By implementing the steps in the preparation, performance, assessment, and fine-tuning stages of "How to Follow Through with Maximum Positive Impact," you will assure yourself that you have done everything possible to

a) Be progressive

b) *stay current* with essential knowledge and skills;

c) best position yourself to convert knowledge and skills into high-quality, on-the-job performance;

d) maintain your ability to perform at the highest level; and

e) stay employable.

CHAPTER SUMMARY

- All *coaching opportunities* are *not equal* in their effectiveness.

- All *coaches* are *not equal* in their effectiveness.

- There is too much inconsistency and ineffectiveness in the quality of coaching.

- This inconsistency and ineffectiveness is unacceptable.

- Prepare, perform, assess, and fine-tune your involvement in receiving coaching, to maximize your learning, retention, and performance.

- Take control of the coaching you need. Ensure that it provides everything you require.

- Along with coaching, there are several other follow-through activities you can incorporate into your life.

- Be *actively involved* in your own follow-through and development. Your ability to remain gainfully employed depends on it.

CALL TO ACTION

1. As mentioned in the Call to Action in the previous chapter, go to Appendix A of this book and order your free copy of the **Well-Being at Work Toolkit**. The toolkit includes the following:

- The Coaching Participant Self-Assessment tool (Figure 6.2)
- The Coaching Participant Self-Assessment Summary: Average of Ten Coaching Sessions Completed tool (Figure 6.3)
- The Coaching Participant Fine-Tuning Action Plan" tool (Figure 6.4)

2. Print, in color, the **Well-Being at Work Quick Reference Card**. Have it laminated at your local office supply store. Keep it visible to help you stay on track.

3. With the quick reference card in hand, prepare for, perform, assess, and fine-tune your actions at your next opportunity for receiving coaching and at every opportunity for receiving coaching from this point forward.

4. Visit www.MPimpact.com to follow and contribute to our blog to stay involved and progressive.

Vigorously *follow through* with maximum positive impact to maximize and maintain your value in the global workforce!

SURVEY

Will I implement the call to action above?
   a) Yes, right now!
   b) No.
   c) Hmm…maybe later.

REFLECTION

To *embed* the knowledge and skills just learned, answer the following questions.

1. *What* did I learn?

    • How can I apply this knowledge to my work?

    • How will it make me more efficient?

    • How can this information help me provide better customer service?

    • How can this insight make me more valuable?

2. *How, when,* and *where* can I *follow through* to stay progressive and maintain these skills? (Practice in my attempt to perfect them.)

3. *How, when,* and *where* can I *apply* the knowledge I acquired and *perform* the skills I have learned?

Chapter 7

Action 3: How to *Perform* with Maximum Positive Impact

*Every individual needs to say: "Not only does my work have
to fit into somebody's global supply chain, but I myself have to
understand how I need to compete and have the skill sets required
to work at a pace that fits the supply chain. And I had better be
able to do that as well or better than anyone else in the world."*
—Vivek Paul

Performance

Consistent on-the-job performance excellence is essential to remaining gainfully employed and staying highly employable. A history of performance excellence is the ticket to getting good, satisfying work when one is in the job market. So performance and productivity must be the DNA of your personal brand.

The Power Unit
(The Power of Three)

You, the Performer

Communication

Learning Provider   **Coach/Mentor**

You, the Performer, the *keystone* of the Power Unit,
are the focus of this action. Your function in this action
is as an on-the-job performer.

You have acquired the specialized knowledge and skills through
learning. You have initiated ongoing *follow-through* with preparation,
practice, and coaching. You have positioned yourself to *perform*.

Knowledge + Skills – Performance = 0

Learning and follow-through are going to pay *huge* dividends when
it's time for you to perform.

What Is Performance?

- Performance is everything.

- Performance is productivity.

- Performance is what is valued.

- Performance keeps you employed.

Performance is the ability to take the knowledge and skills you've learned and use them to do your job superbly. It is about *consistently* doing your job with maximum positive impact. It is about being reliable and responsible. It is about delivering impeccable customer service. It also involves fitting in with your organization's culture. It has to do with being easy to work with. Performance is what counts!

Caring

The first step to world-class performance is caring. Caring deeply about your performance is a prerequisite to delivering highly valuable service. When you care deeply about what you bring to the job, then being just *good enough* is unacceptable. If you do not care deeply about the performance you deliver, everything in this book will probably ring hollow for you. But when you care, it shows. Everyone knows it. Everyone *feels* it. As I mentioned in the preface of this book, in my career, the one thing that has differentiated me from many people is that I always care deeply about my performance and customer satisfaction. When it comes to caring, I can't be beaten. Caring has been my personal differentiator. It has served me well in my career. Let it do the same for you.

The Lesson Introduction

1. **What is "How to *Perform* with Maximum Positive Impact"?**
   "How to *Perform* with Maximum Positive Impact" focuses on what you can do *before*, *during*, and *after* work to ensure that you always

perform with maximum positive impact. It is about taking the knowledge and skills you have attained and applying them with consistent on-the-job performance excellence. It's about being at your best when you must be at your best. And you must be at your best *every day*.

2. **What is its purpose?**

The lesson's purpose is to increase your likelihood of staying gainfully employed if you are currently working. It's about how to perform in preparation for becoming employed. It's about gaining and maintaining income.

3. **Why should I implement this approach?**

You always need to be focused on performance. Things change in a heartbeat. When things do change, you will be in a strong position to maintain employment or gain new employment.

4. **What are the implications of not acting now?**

The danger is that you could potentially get left behind or that you could potentially miss out on a job to someone who is eager, prepared, and passionate about doing your kind of work.

5. **Why should I use *this* particular approach?**

Only good things can happen when you focus on providing world-class value and productivity. Being of service to others is one of life's most noble causes.

6. **What is the evidence that this approach works?**

Invaluable performers tend always to have work. Align yourself with valuable and marketable knowledge and skills. Have proof of your performance history.

7. **What's In It For You? (WIIFY)**

   • Finding good, satisfying work.

   • Keeping good, satisfying work.

   • Finding better, satisfying work.

   • Taking part in a noble cause by helping others find and keep good or more satisfying work.

8. **What are some examples of its practical application?**

   Care deeply about your performance. Show up and deliver a stellar performance every day.

9. **What is the expected outcome?**

   The expected outcome is a gainfully employed, happier, healthier you! Happier, healthier individuals lead to

   • happier, healthier families;

   • happier, healthier communities;

   • happier, healthier countries; and

   • a happier, healthier, safer planet.

   By the end of this chapter, you will have clear direction on how to perform with maximum positive impact, which can only increase your likelihood of acquiring and/or maintaining gainful employment.

How to *Perform* with Maximum Positive Impact

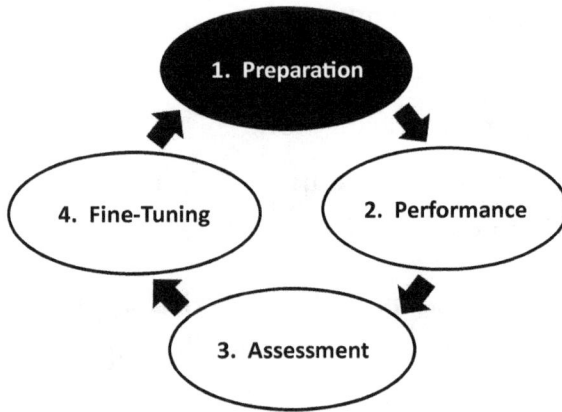

For the final time in this book, we will use the pillar "The Cycle of Excellence" to guide us through this competency.

1. Preparation

The preparation stage of "How to *Perform* with Maximum Positive Impact" is about the things you can do before engaging in the work itself. The purpose of this stage is to help assure you provide stellar on-the-job performance. It's about preparing to perform. Being well prepared makes your job easier. It also significantly reduces your stress level. When you are well prepared, you are not scrambling to get things done. You can complete the job in an organized fashion. Being well prepared is a prerequisite of performance. Nothing will help you deliver world-class performance more than world-class preparation. Nothing will help you with your confidence and the delivery of your expertise more than comprehensive preparation.

You can prepare for the week ahead. You can prepare every morning for the day ahead. Preparation *enables* performance. So without preparation, performance is severely handicapped.

Preparation is not glamorous. Sometimes it can be plodding. But nothing increases the likelihood of stellar performance more than stellar preparation.

This preparation stage is about doing everything you can in preparation for setting new standards of performance excellence.

These words from Abraham Lincoln are a favorite of mine: "Give me six hours to chop down a tree, and I will spend the first four hours sharpening the axe." Hmm…Honest Abe was big on preparation!

So what can *you* do to assure preparedness?

1. **Be there.**

   First and foremost, prepare to show up *early*! Be responsible for being at work early and ready to truly start at the allotted start time. As discussed in a previous chapter, being late affects people down the line. Be the reliable one who can be counted on to get the job done when it needs to be done. Don't be the missing link in the chain. Show up. Show up ready and able to perform.

2. **Manage your time and tasks.**

   Perhaps nothing you can do in the preparation stage is more important than managing your time. Knowing what needs to be done and by when is the first step.

3. **Prioritize.**

   When considering the tasks you are responsible for and the time available, ask yourself the following questions:
   • What *are* the tasks?
   • What needs to be done and by when?
   • What tasks are due soonest?

- What are the most important tasks?
- What are the biggest most time consuming tasks?
- How much time will they take?
- What is the priority for the task?
- Will I need help?
- Will I need other resources?
- Do I know how to do the task?
- Do I have the ability to do the task?
- Do I have the necessary time to do the task?

Tackle the most pressing *big* tasks first—big in this case means the most *important* and the most *urgent*. When it makes sense, tackle the *most difficult* tasks first (if they are a priority). This way, they won't be weighing on you, lurking in your future. The more difficult tasks require your peak energy. Address them when you are at your most energetic.

When others are counting on you to complete a task on time, be sure that you do so. But, of course, things happen. Sometimes things happen that might affect your ability to deliver on time. Once you see this *starting* to occur, let others who might be affected know what is happening and why. Don't make them have to come to you and *ask* you what's going on. Keep them in the loop. This way, they know the situation and can make adjustments of their own that might affect *their* performance. They might even offer you help or advice.

4. **Document it**

The best tool for prioritizing your time is to document your tasks. There are many terrific tools and apps to help you do this. Create a task list. Continuously, *many times throughout your day,* revisit your task list. Ask yourself the following questions:

- How am I doing?
- Has anything changed?
- What do I need to adjust or move?
- How does my timing look?

5. **Assess your tools.**

   What are the tools of your trade? My father always said that the right tool makes a tough job easy. What are the right tools you need to best do your job? Get them. Learn them. Know them inside out. Be a tools-of-your-trade expert.

   Many jobs today involve technology or electronics. The average person uses only a fraction of the capabilities of his or her tools. Dig deep regarding your tools' capabilities. You might find something that will greatly help you in doing a specific task.

   Scan the horizon. Is there a better tool out there? Keep abreast of enhancements of or new releases of your tools. Gain some knowledge about what's new.

   How can you stay on the cutting edge of the technology and tools needed to do your job? What resources will help you do so?

   Keep your tools in top working order. Make sure they are up-to-date and in perfect order to serve you. Care for your tools and maintain them.

6. **Stay mentally and physically sharp.**

   Being at your best requires that you *feel* your best, both mentally and physically. Do what needs to be done in order for you to function to the best of your physical and mental ability. Not being at your best both mentally and physically can have a great impact on your ability to perform.

A big part of staying mentally fit is knowing that you are making a difference. In whatever you do, realize that you are having an influence on a customer with your efforts. Retaining and attaining customers make the world go round. Know that you are a part of the supply chain that keeps customers and gets new ones.

Being of service to others is the noblest of causes. Don't let a lack of energy sabotage your ability to perform. It takes discipline. It is beyond the scope of this book to discuss how you can keep your energy at its peak. Seek guidance regarding health, exercise, and nutrition. For the sake of your well-being, stay mentally and physically fit so that you can perform your job well.

7. **Stay on the cutting edge of your profession.**
   Be *the* go-to expert in the tasks associated with your work. Be the person others come to when they have questions and need advice or guidance. Be the "guru." Prepare for the changes that *will occur* in your profession. See them coming, and make the necessary preparations and adjustments. Alert others to these impending changes. This ability is *highly* valuable to employers and customers alike. I often ask experts about the changes they see on the horizon. The best of the best always have interesting answers. They share their answers with a glint in their eye. They know. They prepare, and they survive!

Have access to resources that will keep you at the cutting edge of your profession. Take classes. Read books and articles. Follow and contribute to blogs. Leave no stone unturned when it comes to staying ahead.

8. **Practice.**

A fine performer I know says, "You have to be great in private before you can be great in public." So true. Practice. Practice before going live. Ideally, you should practice under the watchful eye of your coach. *This* is the time to make mistakes and learn from them. Come up with innovative ways to practice. Make it into a game if you can.

As I prepare for public speaking events, I practice on celebrities. Yes, celebrities! For many years, in magazines, whenever I saw a full-page headshot of a celebrity looking directly into the camera, I'd cut out the photo. I stapled each photo onto a piece of cardboard and then placed my collection of celebrities around my home office. I practice my eye connection by looking directly into the eyes of the celebrity. It is loads of fun and very effective. It is just as effective as practicing face-to-face with live people. I also video myself practicing this way. I then watch my videos and coach myself for the next go-around. I make mistakes, lots of them. But I make them in the harmless confines of my home office.

Be great in private first. Then, go out, go live, and be great in public!

SURVEY

When it comes to being prepared to do my job,
    a) I am always comprehensively prepared.
    b) I'm too busy to prepare.
    c) I figure I can handle whatever comes up.
    d) I could be more prepared than I am.

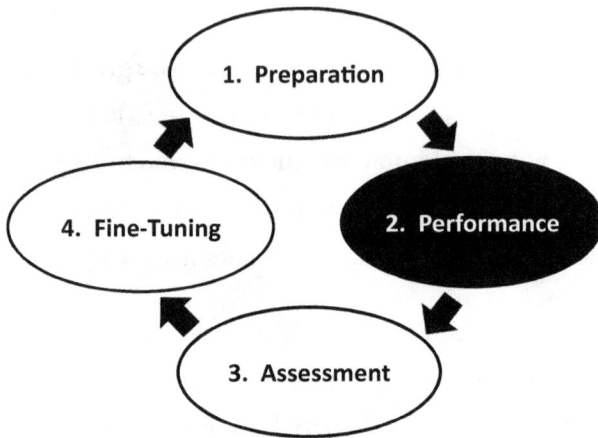

2. Performance

Ninety percent of success is just showing up.
—Woody Allen

To paraphrase Woody Allen, I would add the word *prepared* to the end of his statement.

The performance stage of "How to *Perform* with Maximum Positive Impact" is about *doing* the work. It's the most important concept in this book. It's about delivering, performing, working, and producing. The purpose of this chapter is to give you guidelines to achieve world-class performance. Performance is everything. Potential means you haven't done it yet. Performance is *doing it*.

A Motivating Aspiration

Aspire to *set the new standard of performance excellence* in your specific area of work. You might never achieve such a lofty goal. But by deeply caring and by aspiring and trying to do so, at worst you're likely going to end up performing with excellence. That's still a pretty good place to be.

It's Time to Work

It's time to *showcase your value*, every working hour of every working day. It's time to prove that *nobody is better than you at your profession*. It's time to take pride and to feel satisfaction in knowing that you're delivering the best work of its kind in the world.

So what can you *do*?

Take all of the *knowledge* and *skills* you've acquired,
take all of the *teaching* and *coaching* you've received,
take all of the *preparation* you've undertaken,
take all of your *practice*,

and APPLY it!

A leading professional in his field was once asked how he performs so well under pressure and how he does it so consistently. He replied, "It's easy. I just *do* what I've *prepared* for and *practiced* over and over and over again."

Hmm…sounds like all of your learning, follow-though, preparation, and practice efforts have a payoff—performance excellence! Work-maintaining performance excellence!

So, yes, the payoff, the outcome for all your hard work in learning, follow-through, and preparation is performance ability. Your payoff is that *you* become highly valuable. Your reward in being highly valuable is work security and well-being at work. Your reward is consistent income.

It's about maximizing and maintaining your value in the global workforce.

Here are twelve guidelines to help you perform with maximum positive impact.

1. **Know your job.**

   Know what is required of you. Know this so that you can work at excelling at everything that is expected of you. Thoroughly understand your job description.

   What *is* your job description? What are the *tasks* that must be executed to fulfill your job description? What are the criteria for performing those tasks well above standard? Know exactly what is expected of you. Make sure to ask your employer for a written job description.

   Go online, and take a look at job search websites. Look up positions similar to the one you currently have or to which you aspire. Most ads offer a job description and these will give you a good feel for what is valuable to such a position. See what knowledge and skills are required of others in your area of subject-matter expertise. You will get some good ideas on how to make yourself even more valuable if you acquire the skills and knowledge that perhaps you don't yet possess. Add them to your repertoire.

   If you own, or aspire to own, your own business, what tasks do you need to be great at to succeed in your business? Consider this question as though you were hiring someone to do everything that needs to be done to make your business succeed. What would be included in that job description?

   Once you know your job description, set out to master your ability to perform *all* of the associated tasks. How? Learn, follow through, and perform. Follow *The Actions of Well-Being at Work*.

2. **Delight your customer (Pillar 5)**

First and foremost, your number one focus when it comes to your performance is always the customer. Everything else is secondary. We are *all* in the customer service business. The customer is your employer's most valuable asset and your most valuable asset.

All of us are experts in customer satisfaction, because we are all customers ourselves. We know how we want to be treated when we exchange our hard-earned money for a product or service. We know what it feels like to be treated with respect and cheerfulness. We know, too, what it feels like to be treated the opposite way.

Use your inherent customer service skills with each and every customer. Be memorable to those people in a positive way. Have maximum positive impact on them. Give them a reason to tell others about you and about the memorable, stellar experience you provided them.

Satisfy your customer. *Delight* your customer. Inspire customer loyalty. What is customer loyalty? It's when nothing gets between you and your customers. Even if a better product comes along, they stay with you. Even if a less expensive alternative appears, they stay with you.

It's about you going above and beyond your role in assuring happy, engaged customers. It's about their trust in you. It's about them knowing that *you* are the differentiator. How can you go about inspiring customer loyalty? Exemplary performance always attracts loyalty.

- Focus 100 percent on your customers.
- Listen to them with everything you've got.
- Understand them.

- Smile.
- Sound like you are happy to see them.
- Look like you are happy to see them.
- Sound like you are happy to hear from them.
- Treat them as if they were the most important people in the world.
- Do the little things the average employee would not do.
- Solve their problems (it's when problems arise that you have your best opportunity to inspire customer loyalty).
- *Innovatively* solve their problems.
- If the product or service they purchase involves learning how to use it, take the time to show them how to use it. Go out of your way to help them clearly understand. Show them little tips and tricks that might not appear in instructions. Be the valuable, go-to subject-matter expert in your customers' eyes. They will view you as invaluable and perhaps irreplaceable.
- Stay in touch with them.
- Make it a pleasure for them to buy from you.
- Appreciate them.
- Thank them. *Sincerely* thank them.
- When *they* thank *you*, say, "My pleasure!" Don't say, "No problem." Why bring the word *problem* into it?

We all want to be around people who make us feel good. Make your customers feel good, and they'll come back.

Be a Rainmaker

Want to become invaluable to your employer? Be a *rainmaker*. For most organizations, no one is more valuable than a rainmaker. A rainmaker is a master at customer acquisition.

Want a job for life? Want to make a major contribution to your job security? Become a *master rainmaker.* Be someone who acquires customers for your employer. Without rainmakers, organizations are left with only potential.

Potential – Customers = 0

3. **Affirm the positive.**

Give yourself a pep talk. At the start of every workday, say the following affirmations to yourself:

- Today, I know more than I did yesterday.
- Today, I am going to be of more value than ever before.
- Today, I am going to give it everything I've got.
- Today, I am going to do my best work ever.
- Today, I am going to experience the well-being my work enables.

4. **Actively manage the time and tasks for which you prepared.**

You started this in the preparation stage. As mentioned, keep referring back to your task list many times throughout your day. Reprioritize where necessary. Put a ✔ next to the tasks completed (this feels so good!). Add new tasks as they arise. Ask yourself, "What is my priority *now?*" Look into the future to see what tasks are on the horizon. How will those tasks affect what you're doing now? Might you need to address something *now* in preparation for something coming up in the near future? Then, focus on priorities.

5. **Focus on priorities.**

Yes, *focus* on your priorities. Finish the big, most important, most time-sensitive tasks first. Complete them with all the knowledge,

181

skill, and caring you can muster. Finish the tasks *on time*. Make it a priority to *master your task list*.

6. **Get immersed in your work.**

Have you ever had the experience of getting so absorbed in something that it almost seemed as though you were in a trance? I'm sure you have. You were so concentrating 100 percent on something that nothing else around you seemed to exist. *Time* didn't even seem to exist. Typically, the topic was probably something you were deeply interested in.

Try to get into that *zone* regarding your current task. Stay present. Concentrate on the task at hand. Give it your full attention. Focus. We often do our best work when we are thus immersed. Terrific satisfaction typically follows such concentration.

7. **But Garrett, my work is really boring.**

Make it non-boring! Challenge yourself to make it interesting. Arrange challenges for yourself. Make a productive game out of your work.

I recently started wearing a self-monitoring device on my wrist to help record my steps. I also record what I eat and then log the subsequent calories. Well, I intentionally turned the device on my wrist into "my doubting nemesis," meaning I imagined that the device didn't think I could reach my daily goals. I made it into a competition. Me against it. And it wasn't going to win. I'd show it! I'd meet my step and calorie goals today, and I'd win! This might sound a bit silly, but it is fun, and, for me, it does the trick. I just won't let this device get the best of me.

How can you turn your boring work into a competition or a game? Think outside the box, and have fun with it. It will make a big difference in your daily work experience.

8. **Take a break.**

   Do step away from your work periodically to reenergize and rejuvenate. Try to get some fresh air, if possible. Take some deep breaths. One of my students once said, "We are always three deep breaths away from feeling better." I love it! Get the blood flowing, especially if your work involves sitting most of the time. If your job does involve lot of sitting, consider a standing desk. My very inexpensive, lightweight solution is a nine-dollar plastic moving crate that is thirty-six inches wide by twenty-four inches deep by seventeen inches high. I just plop my monitor, keyboard, and mouse on top of this crate, and I'm in business. It's easy to remove when I feel like sitting.

   Enjoy your breaks in a way that has the most value for you.

9. **Maintain your work environment.**

   A clean, safe, clutter-free work environment can lead to top performance. Keep your work space *productive*. Make it look like your work space means business. Keep your tools or anything you might need readily accessible. Spending time searching for something is not a good use of your time and causes unnecessary stress. Plus, it looks unproductive to anyone who might be able to see what's going on. It doesn't appear professional, so it might be a hit on your credibility.

10. **Stay valuable, and stay employed.**

    Employers pay for value delivered, not for your time. Be valuable. Be invaluable! Constantly hone the value you offer to make sure it remains current and on the cutting edge. Basically, incorporate the skills learned in this book. It's a pretty good recipe to increase your likelihood of remaining gainfully employed.

11. **Don't be high maintenance.**

    Don't be a PITA. Don't be a *pain in the a*** to work with. Instead, be *easy* to work with.

    Fit in with your employer's culture. Talented people who don't conform to an employer's culture find themselves looking for work. I've seen this particular affliction get in the way of the success of too many talented people. Employers (your customers) won't put up with it.

    Don't sabotage your excellent work by being a high-maintenance worker. Don't sabotage your performance or the value you offer with poor or even questionable character. The way one acts can completely ruin one's ability to experience well-being at work.

    Such people who are high maintenance weigh heavily on the individual who is assigned as their manager. Often, a manager decides the "headache" is not worth the bother. Don't be the person who is constantly asking the boss for assistance and guidance. Rather, take responsibility. Don't be the person who issues one complaint after another. Don't be the complainer who is never happy or satisfied. Being this person will make you feel miserable. You don't need such burdens in your life.

If you have a legitimate problem and do not have the authority or the flexibility to make a decision on your own, you can take the following steps:

1. Define the problem.
2. Figure out the cause of the problem.
3. Consider solutions.
4. Discuss with your manager what you feel would be the best solution.
5. Ask for his or her approval to give your solution a try.

Go to your manager with solutions, not problems. Be easy to work with. It will make your work life much more pleasant and a lot less stressful.

12. **Handle change.**

First, expect change. It is coming. Recognize potential obstacles that change might bring. Try to recognize looming change as early as possible so that you can start making adjustments. Those who gracefully handle change are valuable people. They also tend to stay employed and employable.

When change occurs, don't freak out. Receive it with a calm resolve. *Know* you can handle it. Your calm resolve will show others you can handle it. You will also come across as a leader. Keep your eye on the goal, the desired outcome. March triumphantly toward it. I love the words from the iconic poem "If" by Rudyard Kipling: "If you can keep your head when all about you are losing theirs..." What a wonderful sentiment!

Regarding change and how it affects your on-the-job performance, continually ask yourself, "*What* has changed? How might I have to *adjust my performance* to accommodate the change?" And then make those adjustments. Or consider how you might have to *adjust to the change* so that you can *maintain* your current level of performance. Be a change-handling specialist. You'll be using that expertise all the time throughout your career.

A Good, Solid Day's Work

To wrap up this performance stage, feel satisfied with your effort. Know that you gave your work everything you had in the way of knowledge, skill, and effort. Knowing that you put in a good, solid day's work is very satisfying and soothing for the soul.

SURVEY

If you were asked, "*How* or *why* are you valuable in your profession?" what would your response be?
   a) I'd be ready with an accurate answer. I *know* why!
   b) I'd make my answer up on the fly.
   c) I'd have no idea how to answer.
   d) I'm going to work on knowing why.

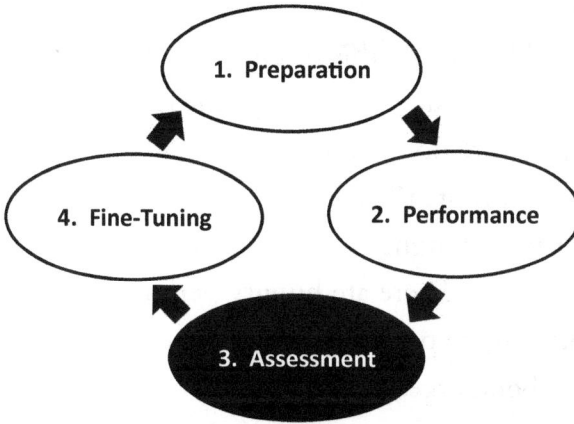

3. Assessment

This is your performance review. Only this is *your* performance review given by *you* for your continued benefit. Don't wait for and rely on a yearly performance review delivered by your employer. Be tougher on yourself than he or she would be. Be brutally honest. Your livelihood and well-being at work depend on it.

The assessment stage of "How to *Perform* with Maximum Positive Impact" deals with assessing your *preparation for work* and your *performance at work* during the just-completed workweek. The purpose of this stage is to make you aware of possible gaps in your preparation and performance that will affect your value. It's important because you need to close those gaps. Continuous improvement is fuel for fine performance.

Acceptable or Exceptional?

The benefit of this stage for you is that it helps you ensure that you *never settle for being just "good enough."* This is an important step in making sure you are doing everything possible to always perform your work tasks *above standard* or *exceptionally*. By the way, it is important to add here that this is not about doing your best. If your best isn't at least at a standard or acceptable level, it's not going to cut it. The world of work does not reward you for effort. Rather, you are rewarded (with staying gainfully employed) by being, at a minimum, *at standard*. I would argue that in this day and age, *at standard* is treading on thin ice. There are hungry performers out there aching for the opportunity to perform. Therefore, to be safe, perform *above standard*. This book urges you to aim for and aspire to perform *well above standard*. Become someone who is representative of the new standard of excellence in your area of expertise. Redefine excellence in your area of expertise. A lofty goal? Yes, it is. You, *the* recognized expert in your field of work? Hey, why *not*? Why not you?

You will use the assessment stage and its tools after a specific work period. As mentioned above, the suggested work period is one week. Yes, evaluate your preparation and your performance based on the just completed week of work, every week.

And remember, as always, ask yourself, "*What did I learn?*"
- What did I learn about my preparation?
- What did I learn about my performance?

Here are the two Performer Self-Assessment tools you can use.

Performer Self-Assessment
Name:
Week Ending Date:
On a scale of 1 to 10, enter a score in the appropriate box **10 = High, True, Often   1 = Low, False, Not Often**

1	I thoroughly *prepared* to perform for the week	0
2	I thoroughly *prepared* to perform for each day	0
3	I arrived early for work each day this week	0
4	I managed my time and tasks expertly	0
5	I documented my time and tasks on a task list	0
6	I maintained the tools of my trade	0
7	My mental and physical fitness was sharp	0
8	I enhanced my position of being on the cutting edge in my area of expertise	0
9	I had an opportunity to practice, and actually practiced some of my core work tasks	0
10	I aspired to set *the new standard of excellence* in my profession	0
11	I performed consistently toward *setting the new standard of excellence*	0
12	I performed my work with world-class excellence	0
13	I focused on the customer	0
14	I focused on the right priorities	0
15	I made my work interesting and enjoyable	0
16	I got maximum benefits from my breaks	0
17	I maintained my work environment	0
18	I was NOT high maintenance, but rather was easy to work with	0
	Overall Performer Self-Assessment AVERAGE	0.0

What did I *learn* about my preparation and on-the-job performance this week?

What did I do well?

For the future I'd like to improve in the area(s) of

What can I do differently to improve my on-the-job performance?

Figure 7.1

	Performer Self-Assessment Summary Average of Ten Weeks											
	On a scale of 1 to 10, enter a score in the appropriate box **10 = High, True, Often 1 = Low, False, Not Often**											
		Week										
	Weeks	1	2	3	4	5	6	7	8	9	10	Avg
1	I thoroughly *prepared* to perform for the week	0	0	0	0	0	0	0	0	0	0	0
2	I thoroughly *prepared* to perform for each day	0	0	0	0	0	0	0	0	0	0	0
3	I arrived early for work each day this week	0	0	0	0	0	0	0	0	0	0	0
4	I managed my time and tasks expertly	0	0	0	0	0	0	0	0	0	0	0
5	I documented my time and tasks on a task list	0	0	0	0	0	0	0	0	0	0	0
6	I maintained the tools of my trade	0	0	0	0	0	0	0	0	0	0	0
7	My mental and physical fitness was sharp	0	0	0	0	0	0	0	0	0	0	0
8	I enhanced my position of being on the cutting edge in my area of expertise	0	0	0	0	0	0	0	0	0	0	0
9	I had an opportunity to practice, and actually practiced some of my core work tasks	0	0	0	0	0	0	0	0	0	0	0
10	I aspired to set *the new standard of excellence* in my profession	0	0	0	0	0	0	0	0	0	0	0
11	I performed consistently toward *setting the new standard of excellence*	0	0	0	0	0	0	0	0	0	0	0
12	I performed my work with world-class excellence	0	0	0	0	0	0	0	0	0	0	0
13	I focused on the customer	0	0	0	0	0	0	0	0	0	0	0
14	I focused on the right priorities	0	0	0	0	0	0	0	0	0	0	0
15	I made my work interesting and enjoyable	0	0	0	0	0	0	0	0	0	0	0

16	I got maximum benefits from my breaks	0	0	0	0	0	0	0	0	0	0	0
17	I maintained my work environment	0	0	0	0	0	0	0	0	0	0	0
18	I was NOT high maintenance, but rather was easy to work with	0	0	0	0	0	0	0	0	0	0	0
	Performer AVERAGE	0	0	0	0	0	0	0	0	0	0	0.00

What did I *learn* about my preparation and performance throughout these ten weeks?

What did I do well?

Over the next 10 weeks, I'd like to improve in the area(s) of

What can I do differently to make my performance even better?

Figure 7.2

This Performance Summary Tool will help you assess yourself over time. How are you doing? By honestly completing these self-assessments you will take a big step toward maximizing your ability to perform.

SURVEY

When it comes to assessing my preparation and performance at work,

    a) I always do it.

    b) I sometimes do it.

    c) I never do it.

    d) I will do it from this point forward.

So what do you do with this assessment information? I'm sure you know by now.

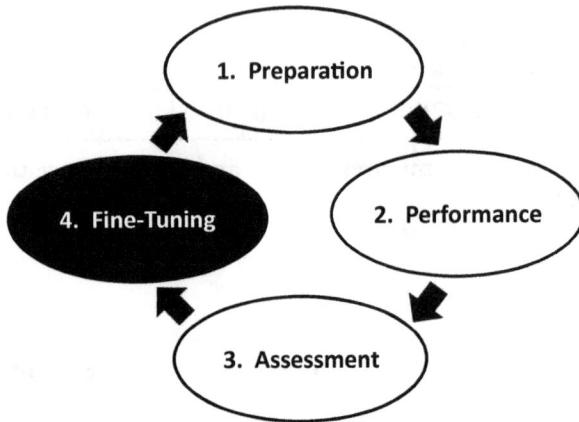

4. Fine-Tuning

As you've done for learning and follow-through, you'll now fine-tune your preparation and performance for "How to *Perform* with Maximum Positive Impact."

What is Maximum Positive Impact Fine-Tuning all about when it comes to your on-the-job performance? It's about the action you take to improve your preparation and performance for the very next opportunity you have to demonstrate your on-the-job expertise. The purpose of this stage, once again, is to ensure that you never settle for "good enough." It's important to you because this is how you continuously grow. The fine-tuning stage ensures that you are even better and more valuable next time (next week). It helps ensure better *results* the next time. Fine-tune after your weekly self-assessment.

Using the results from your self-assessment tools, strategize and fine-tune your approach in both areas. Strategize on the adjustments you will make for your next chance to prepare and perform for your next on-the-job performance opportunity (the coming week).

It's what you *do* with your assessment results that matter.

Let's look at the Performer Fine-Tuning Action Plan tool.

Performer Fine-Tuning Action Plan
Based on: Figure 7.1: Performer Self-Assessment Figure 7.2: Performer Self-Assessment Summary: Average of Ten Weeks
To Fine-Tune My On-The-Job PREPARATION, I will:
Specific action:
Action completion date:
Practice opportunity:
Coach who will observe and provide feedback:
To Fine-Tune On-The-Job PERFORMANCE, I will:
Specific action:
Action completion date:
Practice opportunity:
Coach who will observe and provide feedback:

Figure 7.3

193

SURVEY

Regarding the fine-tuning of my preparation and performance at work
   a) I always do it.
   b) I sometimes do it.
   c) I never do it.
   d) I will do it from this point forward.

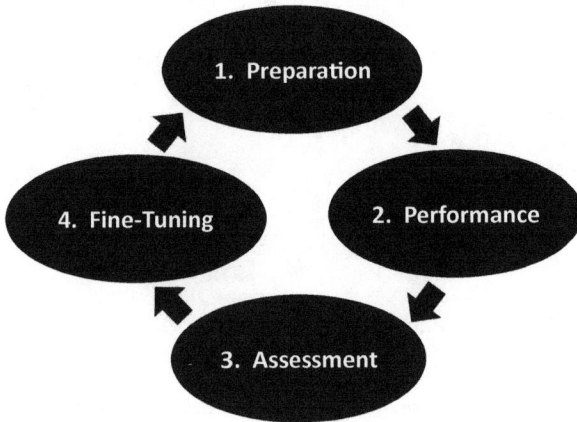

In Closing

By implementing the steps in the preparation, performance, assessment, and fine-tuning stages of the "How to Perform with Maximum Positive Impact" competency, you will position yourself and assure yourself that you have done everything possible to perform with maximum positive impact!

CHAPTER SUMMARY

- The first step to world-class performance is *caring*.

- It all comes down to your on-the-job *performance*.

- *Apply* knowledge and skills learned.

- Be there. Arrive early, prepared to work.

- Manage your time and tasks. Focus on priorities.

- Be mentally and physically ready to perform.

- Practice.

- Aspire to *set the new standard of performance excellence* in your area of specialization.

- The *customer* is always your primary focus.

- Get immersed in your work.

- Stay valuable.

- Don't be high maintenance.

- Be a pleasure to work with.

- Handle change.

- Prepare, perform, assess, and fine-tune your performance to maximize the likelihood that you will stay gainfully employed.

- Be *actively involved* in your own self-assessment and fine-tuning. Remaining gainfully employed will always depend on your on-the-job *performance*.

CALL TO ACTION

1. As a reminder, if you haven't yet done so, go to Appendix A of this book and order your free copy of the **Well-Being at Work Toolkit**. The toolkit includes the following:
    *   The Performer Self-Assessment tool (Figure 7.1)
    *   The Performer Self-Assessment Summary tool (Figure 7.2)
    *   The Performer Fine-Tuning Action Plan tool (Figure 7.3)

2. Print, in color, the **Well-Being at Work Quick Reference Card**. Have it laminated at your local office supply store. Keep it visible to help keep you on track.

3. With the quick reference card in hand, prepare, perform, assess, and fine-tune your on-the-job performance from now on.

4. Visit www.MPimpact.com to follow and contribute to our blog.

Go forth and perform with maximum positive impact from this point forward!

SURVEY

Will I implement the call to action above?
    a) Yes, right now.
    b) Yes, right now!
    c) YES, right now!

REFLECTION

To *embed* the knowledge and skills just learned, answer the following questions.

1. *What* did I learn?

    -   How can I apply this knowledge to my work?

    -   How will it make me more efficient?

    -   How can this information help me provide better customer service?

    -   How can this insight make me more valuable?

2. *How, when,* and *where* can I *follow through* to stay progressive and maintain these skills? (Practice in my attempt to perfect them.)

3. *How, when,* and *where* can I *apply* the knowledge I acquired and *perform* the skills I have learned?

PART 4

Chapter 8

A Strategy for Creating Jobs

There are no new sustainable jobs until there are new customers.
Simply put, the exchange of goods makes everything possible.

To make all of this work perfectly, organizations must focus on the
strengths—the ability to provide consistent, near-perfect performance
in a given activity—of every employee. Not the strengths of the
organization, but the strengths of each individual.

Individuals are the global economy.
Every individual is a source of jobs energy in some way.

—Jim Clifton, The Coming Jobs War

A Movement

It all starts with the individual—an individual working on *purpose*.
A group of individuals working on purpose is a movement. A
movement can change lives.

Unite

1. **What is "A Strategy for Creating Jobs"?**

It is simply that—a *strategy* for creating jobs worldwide. The strategy centers on the already-employed worker. The strategy can be implemented by any individual and any organization.

The premise is that **customers are the key.** Organizations that *retain* their existing customers and consistently *attain* new ones grow. Growing organizations keep people gainfully employed. Growing organizations create jobs and hire people.

- Everyone must embrace a customer-retainment, customer-attainment *mind-set.*
- Everyone must deliver customer-retainment, customer-attainment *performance.*

Learning enables performance. *Follow-through* cements learning. *Performance* attracts customers. Having more customers leads to more *jobs.*

2. **What is its purpose?**

Its purpose is to employ the unemployed and "up-employ" the underemployed.

3. **Why implement this strategy?**

This strategy should be implemented because of the epidemic of joblessness and the despair that causes.

4. **Why implement this particular strategy?**

There is no downside to this strategy. This strategy can only benefit every entity involved. There are no negatives. Organizations, their workforces, their customers, currently unemployed individuals, and our planet will greatly benefit.

5. **What are the implications of not acting now?**
The continuing despair among the unemployed and the underemployed.

6. **Is there evidence that this strategy can work?**
Common sense says that it can. Learning enables and precedes performance. Performance attracts customers. More customers lead to organizational growth and success. Growth and success lead to more jobs.

7. **What's in it for you?**
Once you get employed and contribute to A Strategy for Creating Jobs, it will help you to remain gainfully employed. You would benefit by your employer enjoying organizational growth. The results of the strategy working would contribute to increased job security, a happier workforce, and happier customers. You would enjoy the pride and satisfaction of contributing to a valuable, noble cause.

8. **When will this strategy be used?**
It will be used every day by every individual in the global workforce.

9. **What is the ultimate outcome?**
The ultimate outcome is a greater number of gainfully employed people experiencing well-being at work.

What *Specifically* Needs to Be Done to Make This Strategy Work?

To make this strategy work entails all involved

- becoming *aware* of the strategy;
- *understanding* the strategy;
- *buying into* the strategy;
- understanding the *benefits* of the strategy;
- understanding the *implications* of not solving the job shortage/unemployment crisis,
- completely *buying in* to the strategy by c-level management, line management, and individuals in the workforce;
- *training* (learning) + *coaching* (follow-through) = performance;
- performing *with* maximum positive impact;
- living the customer-retainment, customer-attainment *mind-set*;
- focusing on customer-retainment, customer-attainment *performance*;
- embracing the *Employ the Unemployed* cause; and
- implementing the principles in this book, which provide strategic intervention that will *empower people to perform* with a consistent customer-retainment, customer-attainment mind-set.

Working with a Purpose

People crave *purpose* and *meaning* in their work. To make this a reality for everyone, we propose that organizations do the following:

- *educate* their workforce to have a *customer-retainment/customer-attainment mind-set*
- make this noble cause a commitment to grow their organization and *create jobs* for the unemployed/underemployed

- help their workforce to be *highly engaged* in their *work,* their *customers,* and their *organization* by working together toward the noble cause
- *retain and attain customers* by employees delivering consistent, high-quality, on-the-job performance
- facilitate *collaboration* and *teamwork*
- boost *employee morale* by encouraging everyone to work *with purpose*
- make a *major positive difference* for the people in their organization, their community, their city, their state, and their country

When People Are Employed, They Too Become Customers

When people work, they can more easily afford to buy the things they want. They become customers. Maybe they are new customers for a particular product or service, or perhaps they are returning customers for more products and services. People working contributes to more customers, thus leading to more jobs.

Strategy Advantages

- A new purposeful mind-set
- A *customer-retainment, customer-attainment* mind-set
- Consistent, high-quality, on-the-job performance excellence
- A higher purpose and meaning in one's work
- Part of the job responsibility/description—help employ the unemployed/underemployed

As entities work with the added purpose of *employing the unemployed,* they are *greatly* benefitting themselves.

Strategy Advantages			
For organizations	**For employed individuals**	**For unemployed individuals**	**For cities, states, and countries**
Organizational success and growth - Revenue - Workforce productivity - Morale - Happy, engaged customers - Customer retainment - Customer attainment - Purpose: a contribution to a higher good	**Gainful employment** - Income - Benefits - An increased likelihood of job security - Providing for family - Morale - Self-satisfaction - Pride - Feeling good - Feeling good about getting up and going to work - A sense of well-being - Purpose: a contribution to a higher good - Meaning - We too are customers—a better experience for us when we buy products or services	**Jobs** **Employment for the unemployed and underemployed** - Hope - Their contribution to the strategy when they become employed - We too are customers—a better experience for us when we buy products or services	**Jobs** **Lower unemployment numbers** - Lower unemployment benefits are distributed - Money savings - Higher satisfaction ratings for government officials - Higher gross domestic product - Increased exchange of goods and services for money, leading to **a stronger economy**

Heroes

The heroes whom organizations need in today's ultracompetitive world are individuals who *inspire, enable,* and *encourage* people to *perform* with maximum positive impact.

The hero is *you*.

Inspire, enable, and *encourage* others to

- truly acquire essential knowledge and skills through continuous learning;
- convert knowledge and skills into high-quality on-the-job performance via ongoing follow-through;
- maintain performance excellence;
- retain and attain customers through impeccable customer service;
- help employ the unemployed; and
- help up-employ the underemployed.

Then, you will truly be a hero.

A New Hire—Celebrate the Occasion

Every time your organization or department hires someone, *stop!*

- Celebrate!
- Savor the moment.
- Recognize the accomplishment.
- Make it a ceremony.
- Welcome and embrace the individual.
- Embrace the satisfaction of knowing that your efforts bore fruit.
- Hail one fewer unemployed soul.

Those Within Can Help Those Without

Those within the "walls of employment" can help those without employment. It won't cost you a dime, and it will make a lot of people very happy, including you.

People *within* can help people *without*. Invite them in. Make a place for people who are on the outside looking in. Make a difference. If not *you*, who? If not *now*, when?

CHAPTER SUMMARY

- Let's all work together to help get others employed.

- *You* can contribute to a Strategy for Creating Jobs.

- *You* can make a major difference by doing your small part.

CALL TO ACTION

1. Do your part to help get others employed.

2. Focus on retaining customers.

3. Focus on attaining customers.

4. Visit www.MPimpact.com to follow and contribute to our blog.

Conclusion

The likelihood of finding, keeping, and thriving in rewarding employment is increased by a healthy combination of

- a strong desire for well-being at work;
- You Enterprises;
- the pillars;
- learning;
- following through; and
- performing.

Follow-Through

Learning – Follow-through = 0

It is *not* the knowledge and skills you possess but the action you take based on your knowledge and skills that will determine your outcomes. When you are presented with new information, you always have a choice to make. You can either do something with that information, or you can ignore it. What will *you* do?

Now it's time for you to follow through on the actions covered in this book. How *will* you follow through with what you learned here?

1. Use what you learned in the lesson "*How to Follow Through with Maximum Positive Impact.*"
2. Use your *Power Unit.*
3. Use the *Maximum Positive Impact Goal-Achieving Formula.*
4. Use the *tools* provided at the end of the "Action" lessons.

A combination of the above will help you truly implement what you've learned in this book.

Follow through!

Separate Yourself from the Masses

You need an edge on your competition. Separate yourself from the others who want your job. Maybe the other person out there doesn't make the most of his or her learning opportunities—but you do. Maybe the other person does not follow through with what he or she has learned—but you do. Maybe the person who wants your job thinks a just "good-enough" performance is good enough—but not you. Separate yourself from the masses.

Implementing the competencies in this book will

- contribute to your overall well-being; and
- give you maximum positive impact *value.*

Sometimes it's the smallest of margins that separates the person who got the job from the person who didn't. Sometimes it's the smallest of margins that separates the person who *keeps* the job from the person who didn't. Don't leave this to chance. Do whatever you can to make sure you are offering value that is second to none.

Focus on customer retainment and attainment. Be invaluable. Take pride in your contribution to "A Strategy for Creating Jobs."

So, in conclusion, get out there and *take action*. Get out there and *make your contribution* to a happier, healthier, safer planet. You, your family, and your fellow inhabitants of our beautiful planet will benefit greatly.

Have maximum positive impact on everyone around you, and the world will be a better place.

APPENDIX

Appendix A

The Well-Being at Work Toolkit

S end an e-mail requesting your free **Well-Being at Work Toolkit** to **WAWtoolkit@MPimpact.com,** and we will be happy to send you electronic versions of the following:

1) A Well-Being at Work Quick Reference Card

2) The Maximum Positive Impact Goal-Achieving Formula

3) Learner Tools
   • Well in Advance of the Learning Event—Presession Checklist
   • Learner Self-Assessment
   • Learner Self-Assessment Summary
   • Learner Fine-Tuning Action Plan

4) Coaching Participant Tools
- Coaching Participant Self-Assessment
- Coaching Participant Self-Assessment Summary
- Coaching Participant Fine-Tuning Action Plan

5) Performer Tools
- Performer Self-Assessment
- Performer Self-Assessment Summary
- Performer Fine-Tuning Action Plan

6) Template for the "You Need, I Offer" letter

7) The Hierarchy of Well-Being at Work

8) The Cycle of Well-Being at Work

Appendix B

Bibliography

These books have inspired and guided me to achieve well-being at work.

– Carnegie, Dale. 1936 *How to Win Friends and Influence People.* New York: Simon & Schuster

– Carnegie, Dale. 1944. *How to Stop Worrying and Start Living.* New York: Simon & Schuster

– Clifton, Jim. 2011. *The Coming Jobs War.* New York: GALLUP PRESS

– Colvin, Geoff. 2008. *Talent is Overrated.* London, England: Penguin Group

– Dweck, Carol S. 2006. *Mindset.* New York: Random House

– Friedman, Thomas L. 2005. *The World Is Flat.* New York: Farrar, Straus and Giroux

– Pink, Daniel H. 2005. *A Whole New Mind.* New York: RIVER-HEAD BOOKS

– Pink, Daniel H. 2009. *Drive.* New York: RIVERHEAD BOOKS

Index

You can connect with Garrett through the Maximum Positive Impact, Inc. website at **www.MPimpact.com**.

www.ingramcontent.com/pod-product-compliance
Lightning Source LLC
Chambersburg PA
CBHW060007210326
41520CB00009B/852